FISHERS OF MEN

Mark 1:17—Then Jesus said to them, "Follow Me, and I will make you become fishers of men."

Brian Thomas Ellis

**A Missionary Biography and Recount
of God's Work of Reformation in the Reformed Baptist Churches
of the Philippines**

ISBN 978-1-312-32409-1
Imprint: Lulu.com

Full-color paperback, variorum edition.

Editor: Jose A. Fadul
Associate Editors: Eunice G. Ellis, Rebecca L. Macapagal, Ian M. Densham
Layout and Cover Design by the Editor

Fishers of Men

Brian Thomas Ellis

A Missionary Biography
and Recount of God's Work of Reformation
in the Reformed Baptist Churches
of the Philippines

Brian & Necy Ellis

Missionaries to the Philippines

Necy and I met in Singapore in 1966 for my language study and looking where to go for my missionary assignment. We began our missionary journey together in Lubang Island, Occidental Mindoro, Philippines, shortly after our wedding in April 1968.

In 1977, we moved to Cubao, Quezon City and started a literature ministry of what is now The Evangelical Outreach, Inc. Then in 1979, the Lord providentially led us to establish Cubao Reformed Baptist Church, then Grace Ministerial Academy for the training of men for the ministry.

In 1995, the Christian Compassion Ministries was founded, an orphanage for boys and girls. Then the Drop-in-Center for the homeless or street people followed sometime later.

May all the glory be given to God who chooses people for the work of His grace.

CONTENTS

Foreword

by Pastor Ramon Macapagal
Cubao Reformed Baptist Church

Brian Thomas Ellis, *"Instrument in the hand of God"*

There was an influx of university students in 1979 through 1984 in Cubao Reformed Baptist Church (CRBC). The first *local* CRBC pastor, George Capaque (who was a deacon then), was instrumental in bringing these students from Inter-Varsity Christian Fellowship (IVCF). I was one of those students, and in the providence of God, I became a member of the church in 1983. I was then in my early twenties, while Pastor Brian Ellis was in his early forties. The church gathered in the house of Brian and Necy at 55 Miami Street, Cubao, Quezon City. I was privileged to sit under the ministry of Pastor Ellis. He preached in both Tagalog (local dialect) and English (British English). It was my first time to learn the Doctrines of Grace and sing the hymns from Grace Hymnbook. It brought a personal revival to me.

Pastor Brian Ellis has been part of the highlights of my life. November 28, 1987 was my marriage to Rebecca Limbago, which Pastor Ellis officiated. The Lord blessed us with three lovely daughters: Tabitha Anne, Riva Elizabeth, and Thea Monique. Pastor Ellis spoke during the thanksgiving celebrations in each of their birthdays as well.

In 1987, I was ordained as one of the deacons of CRBC, and did the tasks assigned to the diaconate until 1994 when, at this period, Brian saw the need for a co-Elder to carry the burden of the ministry. I was so challenged by Brian to consider the ministry as he was very confident that I was "called to the ministry". Reluctant as I was, I began praying about it. By the Lord's providence, I was ordained as a Pastor in May 1994. Brian mentored me to the work of the ministry. But it was difficult for me at that time, as I still have a secular business to attend to and the church could not afford to financially support a full-time Elder then. I was in a crossroad. The church was growing, and the demands were increasing. I had to choose whether to leave my secular work and become full time in the ministry, or step down as Elder and concentrate on my secular work. My wife Rebecca prayed with me and resolved to take a step of faith for the sake of the church: a journey that starts with that first step along with the desire to achieve something, even if you can't totally see it yet.

At first, it was also difficult working with Brian as his co-Elder. The reasons are understandable. First, Brian still sees me as the young man who needed guidance. Secondly, it was difficult for a student-teacher to work as a co-equal. Thirdly, I was inexperienced to the work of the ministry. But Brian was patient with me and soon, we worked together as co-Elders. I appreciated his graciousness in eventually accepting me as his co-equal in the ministry. We made the journey by taking each day step by step and then repeating it again until we reach our destination.

Brian maintained a missionary's heart. So, he still gave himself in helping establish reformed churches in different places. I found myself focusing on the oversight of most of the matters and dealings of the church. I could not forget how Pastor Ellis saw my need, as well as for other men's need for some further training in the pastoral ministry. This prompted him and Pastor Noel Espinosa to start Grace Ministerial Academy (GMA) in 1996. This academy is still standing today in its 27th year.

The church grew rapidly and the need for more Elders became evident. In the Lord's goodness, another Elder in the person of Ismael Montejo Jr., was ordained to the ministry in 2006. Then, after 15 years, a very able young man graduated from GMA, Joseph Mangahas, and he was added to the Eldership in 2019. Earlier in 2016, Pastor Ellis had a coronary artery bypass surgery, and afterwards began having memory problems, particularly remembering recent events. It was at this point that Pastor Ellis saw his time to retire from the ministry. It was in the year 2020—the year when church and other group meetings were restricted by the government due to the Covid-19 Pandemic, when he formally stepped down as pastor of CRBC. We gave him a tribute for his legacy as "Instrument in the hand of God" during our 43rd Church Anniversary.

What a man of God indeed! He was greatly used by God at the start of the Reformation work all over the Philippines. Today, there are about a hundred reformed churches established. Pastor Brian Ellis can confidently say with the apostle Paul, *"I have fought the good fight, I have finished the race, I have kept the faith. Henceforth there is laid up for me the crown of righteousness, which the Lord, the righteous judge, will award to me on that day, and not only to me but also to all who have loved his appearing."* 2 Timothy 4:7-8.

To all these, all glory to God.

I am turning 64 years old in August of this year 2023. I have been in the ministry for almost three decades. I see myself likewise retiring from the ministry--well into the future. *Great missionaries and pastors come and go but God remains, and the church of Christ will remain until Christ returns in his glory.*

I would like to acknowledge Wattisham Baptist Church in Ipswich, Suffolk, England--the sending church of Pastor Brian Ellis. The Wattisham Baptist Chapel is a fairly remote place, up in the hills beside a large airfield which cuts it off from its nearest neighbors. I realized how much they supported Brian until now. CRBC was greatly privileged to be the recipient of the generosity of the brethren at Wattisham. I could not forget when their Pastor, the late Gordon David Hawkins came to inaugurate our building at 21 Harvard Street in August 1986. Indeed, all throughout, they have never stopped supporting us as a church until now. They are truly partners in the vineyard of the Lord. Praise be unto God!

The memoirs of Pastor Brian Ellis will surely leave an indelible mark in the history of the church. To this purpose, his life's ministerial biography is written for the Lord Jesus Christ's glory.

MAP OF THE PHILIPPINES

Batanes

South China Sea

Ilocos Norte

Cagayan

Ilocos Sur

La Union

LUZON

Pangasinan

Zambales

Manila

Bataan

Batangas

LUBANG ISLANDS

LUBANG

BATANGAS

ORIENTAL
MINDORO

**OCCIDENTAL
MINDORO**

Mindoro

Philippine Sea

VISAYAS

Samar

Panay

Cebu

Palawan

MINDANAO

Brian Thomas Ellis

CHAPTER 1

FISHING IN LUBANG ISLAND

I ran as fast I could on the jagged rocks of the reef. The black clouds of the squall were fast approaching from the East, and we needed to get off from that reef before the wind and the rain hit us. Necy had already gone towards the beach along the reef, but I had left our canoe out on the end of the reef. I reached the small outrigger canoe and pushed off into the lagoon and began to paddle as fast as I could towards the beach about two hundred yards away. I reached about halfway when the squall hit. The wind was fierce with driving rain. Suddenly the sea which had been calm was a like a cauldron. The fierce wind came from behind my small frail canoe. I drove my paddle as hard as I could into the water and paddled for all my worth. I could see that Necy had reached the shelter of a small, thatched hut on the beach and had turned to watch my progress, but I seemed to be getting nowhere. As I thrust and plunged with my paddle, I could see my wife laughing although my glasses were covered with water from the rain. Looking down I realized the reason for her laughing. The canoe was filled with water, no, it was under the water, and I was still sitting in it! I was the only part of it remaining above the surface as I tried to paddle furiously for the beach. There was nothing more to do but swim for it and tow the canoe behind me.

This was a glimpse of our life, Necy and I, where we lived on the island of Lubang. This is where we had moved as missionaries one month after our marriage in 1968. Lubang is a coastal municipality and one of a small group of islands in the Philippines –situated about 60 miles from Manila out into the South China Sea. It is the largest island in the Lubang Group of Islands, an archipelago that lies to the northwest of the northern end of Mindoro. The island is divided into two municipalities: Lubang and Looc. The large settlement town is Lubang, and the town center is about 8 miles or 13 kilometers northwest of Tilik Port.

Fishing was one of the main livelihoods of the men of Tilik, on Lubang Island aside from planting rice, garlic, peanuts, and vegetables. All the villages were concentrated on the beaches of the island. These provide food and a living for many of the men particularly for those who do not have access to wet rice field paddys. During the monsoon season they may grow dry hillside rice, depending upon the abundant rain but for most of the year, the weather permitting they would fish to get food for their families and hopefully enough to sell to pay for the basic needs of their families.

Living in a fishing village, it was natural to go out with the men fishing to get to know them and to experience their way of life. Ka Sining, the old man with one leg who attended our Lord's Day services regularly was the first to take me out fishing.

We went out in a small outrigger canoe into the lagoon where Tilik is located. There was a long reef that protected the lagoon from the heavy waves. Here we fished not far off the second reef that jutted out into the center of the lagoon from the shore and almost divided the lagoon into two. We were fishing for *bisugo*. A small fish about 6 to 9 inches long, easily recognized because of its red and white stripes like a zebra. One uses a small hand-held line and a small hook to catch a few fish, which would be enough for lunch.

One early morning, we were awakened with a banging on our front door downstairs and a voice calling us. I groped for the flashlight and looked at the bedside clock. It was about two o'clock in the morning! We stumbled out of bed and made our way to the front door recognizing the voice of our neighbor. It was not an emergency, no one was sick and needed driving to the hospital and no one had died! He had caught some fish and especially some *talakitok* (jack or trevally in English), and he knew we loved this excellent-tasting fish so on his arrival home at 2:00 a.m., he immediately called us. We were given the fish and Necy would pay later in the day. Now, she had to start cleaning this excellent catch even if it was two o'clock in the morning!

The real fishing takes place outside of the lagoon in the deep water beyond. *Mang Panching* was the expert here, but he only fished alone. Yet as I got to know him, he agreed to take me along. He knew all the coral heads out in the deep water and by lining up the hills on the island and then across to the high island of Ambil he could find those coral heads, which shelter the shoals of fish. The method of fishing was again handheld line but this time it was the *kuskus*. The *kuskus* is a line with at least twenty hooks often over thirty, usually on wire traces because of *tikil*, a fish with razor sharp teeth, which would part any nylon. There was no bait, but lures on each hook made from white chicken feathers or if the person had access to an old rubber tire, the white silken threads that were used to strengthen the tire. The whole line was let down on a weight which reached the bottom and then the line was pulled up and down steadily to make the white lures move. Often, we would hit a school of fish and we might catch as many as ten or even fifteen fish at one time. This was really fishing and was great fun.

One day as we were out, we suddenly saw fish jumping off to the left. There was a large school of anchovies, small minnows about two to three inches long. There must have been hundreds of thousands and hunting them were Tuna. Quickly our lines were hauled in, the motor started and the *kuskus* exchanged for one spinning lure. We were after tuna. With the motor flat out our out-rigger motorboat bounced across the water as we chased the shoal of fish. The first one struck and was hauled in. A yellow fin tuna about two and a half feet long. As soon as it was in the boat it bled and was dead within minutes. But we had no time, the line was back in the water and the next one bit. Three tunas in as many minutes but the next was not tuna. It was a large fish longer than the tuna but was useless as an eating fish. The next was the same and Mang Panching cut back on the throttle. He was not going to waste gas chasing these fish that no one could eat because of the taste. Yet it had been an exciting and profitable day fishing in deep water.

But there were other ways of fishing. There was the '*dala*', a throwing net seen all over the world, like that used by the disciples in the Sea of Galilee. Here one stalks in the shallows looking for the sight of fish or shrimp and then casts the net quickly from the shoulder. It spreads out in a huge circle hopefully ensnaring the fish that was seen.

Then the '*pukot*', a large net that is usually drawn out from the beach by men rowing a large outrigger boat. It is drawn in a huge half circle and then hauled to shore. A large bag on the end traps all the fish. Another variation is without the bag, and this is used in shallow waters. Our last home in Tilik was just off the beach and we were roused one morning by the shouts of the men. I rushed to the beach and was able to help in pulling in the net. One of the problems was that a lot of *barnak*, a delicious shallow water fish had been entrapped in the circle of the net, but they could jump the net to get out. The net had to be brought together as quickly as possible to stop this happening and the water pounded to frighten the fish into getting entangled in the net. I got my shorts wet rushing with the other men, but I went home with several *barnak* which is my portion of the catch I had helped save.

Sometimes we would stretch out at night a shallow net in water about one meter deep. This would be about 100 yards long and then we men who were out would pound the water with paddles and walk towards the net driving any fish into the net. The night I tried this we caught very little.

Virling Tria

One of my close friends was Virling Tria, his wife was the first convert in Tilik. Virling eventually made a profession of faith in Christ and was baptized but his profession was always rather erratic, and he was never a strong Christian. Virling was a tailor by trade, but he eventually got a job in the post office, a government position, which meant a regular salary. Virling and I used to go out during April and May, fishing in shallow water with a lantern. During those two months just prior to the monsoon season the prevailing winds would die away and the sea would be as calm and smooth as a mirror. At night we would take a pressure lantern and wade almost up to our waists. One of us would have a small round net on a handle (like a butterfly net) but not for

3

catching butterflies. The other would carry a three-pronged spear, which was used on a homemade spear gun. We were hunting shrimp, crab, fish and anything edible. The eyes of the shrimps would glow in the light from the lantern. The secret was to place the circular net a little way from the shrimp without scaring it and then the other to move their foot slowly up behind the shrimp causing it to shoot off in the other direction hopefully straight into the net. We always seemed to get a good bag of shrimps enough for Virling's family and Necy and me. The spear gun came in handy for small fish and occasionally we would get quite a good-sized edible crab. One night we wasted quite a while trying to catch a large foot-long squid which always saw us coming and was too much of a match for us. Indeed, squids are generally very fast.

The fishing in the village was almost always of these varieties until someone in the village purchased a 'basnig' and based it there. A '*basnig*' is again an outrigger boat but would be 30 feet or more in length. It was equipped with a generator and had large lights on the bow and stern and down the side of the boat. Fishing was by a large circular net which is let down under the boat and then the lights are turned on to attract the fish. Gradually the lights are turned off until one spotlight is left on in the center of the boat. This is then dimmed drawing the fish up the surface while the net is also hauled up. The plan is to catch the shoals of small fish, and squid, which abound. When the net is brought up it is usually swarming with fish. During the interval between lowering of the net the men fish with hand lines. Usually, the kuskus is used to catch the large fish. The night I was out I had no kuskus, so I used a large hook. Soon I was hauling in several large red rockfish, the largest was about 10 lbs. in weight. However, I am very much a 'land lover' and as the sea got up to rather a swell my stomach began to tell me that land was much preferable to the ocean. I laid down inside the small cabin on the boat waiting until the time the men would eventually head for home. As dawn arrived, we headed for Tilik and the news in the village was that I had caught a lot of fish as I proudly walked down the main street hardly being able to carry all the fish strung together from my nights fishing.

Yet we were not in Tilik to catch fish. We were there to catch *men*.

CHAPTER 2

THE BEGINNING

BECOMING A MISSIONARY IN THE FAR EAST

I, Brian Thomas Ellis born on 19 September 1938, at Ealing, London, left England to become a missionary in the Far East in 1966. I had attended several meetings of the Overseas Missionary Fellowship (the former China Inland Mission) and believed the Lord was calling me to go overseas. Following Bible School in Scotland where I studied at the Bible Training Institute, I applied to the OMF to become a missionary. I was thinking initially of possibly working in Thailand or even Japan.

Following an interview with the OMF Board, I was accepted for a missionary course at their headquarters in Newington Green, North London. After that I was accepted to go to the Far East. So along with a few other new recruits including a good friend Alan Ellard from Bible College we made for Tilbury Docks to board the large passenger liner Orcades to make the long journey to Singapore.

Brian Thomas Ellis

The trip was excellent. We stayed for half a day in Holland where we took on more passengers, and then we made our way past the Rock of Gibraltar on to Piraeus and Athens in Greece. It was a wonderful stop over. To stand where the Apostle Paul had stood and preached the gospel to the Athenians. A city of the ages. We did not have a lot of time but most of the day we were able to spend in Athens and climb up the Acropolis and visit some of the temples and places Paul would have seen. Again, we took on more passengers who were Greeks going to Australia, to create or achieve a new life there.

Our trip continued through the Suez Canal where we had only a little time to stop so we were unable to visit the Pyramids but did get to go into a Muslim temple. We did stop in Aden for supplies but could not go ashore due to some shooting going on the previous day. The next day we began the long voyage across the Indian Ocean to Bombay. We were met at Bombay pier by an employee of Pilkington Glass.

I had worked for some time with one of the Directors of Pilkington Glass in Norfolk and my mother worked in their home. So, several of us had a tour of Bombay by car. The thing I remember most was going into a Jainist Temple and seeking this ugly statue with several arms. I could not stay in the temple I had to get out, as all I could feel was the presence of evil. Well, we left Bombay for the long journey to Malaysia, where we stopped at the island of Penang for the day. Then it was onward to our destination in Singapore. The P&O Liner Orcades was then going on further to Australia.

How good God is to His people! To be able to see different places and countries and to spend time in some of those lands. I was to spend at least 3 months in Singapore where something very special happened to me.

LANGUAGE SCHOOL AND MEETING MY WIFE TO BE

I arrived in Singapore on April 20, 1966, after a 3-week sea voyage on the P&O Liner Orcades. I was one of the new missionary recruits from England and Europe. On that day I first met my wife to be, although I was not, of course, aware of it at the time. She, along with missionaries from the Overseas Missionary Fellowship Headquarters and Language School were there to meet the ship from England. She was Eunice Goco or Necy as everyone called her, a Filipina who was destined to be my language teacher for the next four months in the Language Center of the Overseas Missionary Fellowship (OMF) in Singapore.

Those first few days in Singapore, determined many things under God, for what was to be for the rest of my life. After I settled into the Language School, I had a couple of days of interviews by Arnold Lee and Dennis Lane, the mission directors. The world headquarters of OMF was and is still in Singapore. I was interviewed and asked about my convictions as to which country the Lord was leading me. I had originally thought it might be Japan, this was after reading some books on the work there, but that had faded after hearing some missionaries' stories whilst they were on furlough. My leanings were then to Laos—a little-known country near Northeast Thailand.

I was quickly told that with my particular church beliefs, which I had come to hold during the last few years, would not fit in Laos where the churches were mainly of a "Plymouth" Brethren structure. Northeast Thailand (Laos) was out, the Mission only had two older ladies working there and I could not work under them. No! I should go to the Philippines where the form of the churches that the OMF were planting would be much more in accord or match with my own beliefs. "We will give you two days to pray about it!"

That decision would affect the rest of my life. Only two days to reach a decision, so I took it to the Lord. The Lord's ways are past finding out. At the end of the two days, I agreed to be assigned to the Philippines. I was not so happy with the decision, but I went along with it and began to study Tagalog. Tagalog is the national language of the Philippines and one of the eight major dialects spoken there. Also, the country has about 7,641 islands, and about 120 to 175 spoken languages. Knowing Tagalog is very important; however, I am grateful that English is widely spoken there as English and Tagalog are the official languages in the Philippines.

Not only did Eunice Goco or Necy become my language teacher, but she was also to be my co-teacher at the church we both attended in Singapore. She went there because it was the church of a pen pal of one of her sisters. I was assigned to attend the same church in Queenstown by the OMF and to be of use in the Sunday School. Now a Filipina in those days would never travel alone but needed a companion. Not only did I attend the same church and teach in the same Sunday School, but I also escorted Miss Necy Goco, who never travelled alone. In addition to going on the Lord's Day, we went there during the week for the Sunday School Teachers meeting. During the day, I spent several hours in the classroom with Necy and at least one hour practicing Tagalog with her. Over those next four months, we fell in love.

Eunice 'Necy' Goco

At the end of August, I moved on to further language study in the Philippines while Necy remained to teach the next batch of students and help run the language center. We corresponded with each other while I continued my language study and got to know the people the Lord has set me to do His mission work within the Philippines.

OFF TO THE PHILIPPINES

Ann Judge, Elvie Gailitis, myself, and three new other missionaries to the Philippines board a French ship from Singapore to Manila in August 1966. The boat was okay but not half as good as the P & O Liner from England. I shared my cabin with a Roman Catholic priest who as a missionary was on his way to Japan, I believe. We did not talk much as his English was not so good and my French was even worse.

The only thing I seem to remember of that voyage were the bathroom being awash with water all the time and the food coming in small portions on various plates. The French way I gather. We did however have the privilege of stopping in Bangkok for one day and were given a very fine tour by the OMF missionary staff there. It consisted of a water trip up the maze of waterways that make up part of Bangkok and seeing how parts of Asia live. We visited the king's palace, the royal barges, and the Temple of the Dawn. We were conscious again of the darkness of paganism (here Buddhism) with so much money lavished on these temples, with their gold-coated spires and statues of devils guarding their entrances. The people of Thailand are very religious with elaborately painted and tiled roofs, and temples with gold-covered spires which adorn temples in the simplest of villages. It is a religion without true knowledge. How we must thank God for our Christian heritage in the West although so many today have thrown it away.

In 1974 I had the privilege of visiting Thailand for a month and visiting with missionaries in the villages of central Thailand. I remember one home where we went to pray and read the Bible. The young woman probably in her late teens or early twenties had a stomach as large as any pregnant woman, but this was not pregnancy it was a malignant tumor. She just sat there her face painted white. The missionary prayed, read the Scriptures, and sought to witness to her and the family of Christ the Savior. Yet he was just one of the many religions who came to the house. There was no hope in that home, just darkness and fatalism to the terrible fact of death slowly approaching. What it means to be without the Lord Jesus Christ! I also met Mr. Yu a leprosy patient and preacher of the gospel. I attended a meeting of Pastors where he was one of the speakers. When he stood up the first thing one noticed is that he had no fingers, this was the result of leprosy. He turned the pages of his Bible by means of rubber bands, which were wrapped around his hands. He was able to drag his stumps across the pages and with these pieces of rubber to turn the pages. The missionary told me his testimony as he spoke. Because he had leprosy, he was taken to the Christian Hospital at Manoram, and there while a patient in the leprosy ward he heard about the Lord Jesus Christ who came to die for sinners. "I thank God that I have no hands", he said, "because I have no hands, I came to hear the gospel and to know the Lord Jesus, my Savior."

A couple of days after our visit to Bangkok we arrived in the Philippines during the tail end of a typhoon. There was not much room, but it rained constantly. We were met and taken to the Manila Mission Home of the OMF. To get into the home we had to wade through floodwaters from the gate, the result of the typhoon. The Home itself was a large concrete building built on pillars about five feet from the ground and so above the floodwaters.

I remember a similar situation several years later when during typhoon "Yoling" we were in Manila at the Mission Home. The flooding was far worse then, and many phone lines were down. The manager of the home was concerned about several missionaries who lived over a mile from the Pasig River. The two of us decided to walk to find out how they were. We walked through flood waters. At one point we thought we would have to swim as the water came up to our necks and we passed cars and a taxi at the side of the road completely underwater. Upon reaching the homes of the missionaries, people in one-story homes had vacated and moved to the home of one of the missionaries who had two floors and so they were encamped on the second floor, the first floor and all their homes were under several feet of water.

Man thinks he is so powerful but who are we compared to God? We are nothing and we tremble at the earthquake and the storm!

The afternoon following our arrival in Manila from Singapore, (Manila is the capital city of the Philippines) we were met by Necy's brother-in-law, Bert Espiritu. He has taken us through the flood waters by taxi to visit his family. His small home was also under water, and we crossed from the doorway through the living room to the stairs on planks of wood. We were then entertained to a meal upstairs in one of the bedrooms.

The next two days we spent at the immigration where we had our first taste of Philippine red tape. We had to acquire 27 signatures on the various documents we needed to stay in the country as well as "play the piano", that is, have our fingerprints taken.

As soon as immigration was finished, we were taken by Brian Gibson who was then the Acting Superintendent that year to Batangas City on the bus. We were placed on an old boat for our ride to Calapan (Necy's hometown) in Oriental Mindoro. The bus was an event in itself. It had no door or gangway down the middle of the bus. In fact, you climbed up the outside of the bus, which was all open on one side and then sat on one of the benches which went from one side of the bus to the other. People kept squashing in more and more on to those benches with everything you can think of going under the bench including live chickens with their feet tied together. The only protection from the rain, which continued to fall, was a canvas awning that covered that side. The poor bus conductor had to swing along this open side, in constant danger of his life, to collect the passengers' fares. He would first go the whole length of the bus issuing tickets and then start again collecting money from all the passengers. He did all this while having his arm wrapped around a post of the bus, notes deftly wrapped around his fingers. The road was only tarmacked for about 25 miles from Manila and the rest of the way to Batangas City was on a pot-holed dirt road. (Thirty years later, things have much changed, with two lanes either side on a Toll Way now, for all those miles to Batangas City.)

After a three-hour boat ride to Calapan, our luggage consisting of boxes and cases were loaded on to the mission jeep, while we the passengers, got to ride on a *calesa* (a horse-drawn, two-wheeled cart with a roof) for the half-mile (a little less than a kilometer) ride to the Mission Home.

CHAPTER 3

FIRST TWO YEARS

CALAPAN

In those days Calapan seemed to me to be like a wild west town, small dusty and backward. My life there consisted of daily language study with a language teacher, private study often listening to language tapes and then two hours a day, during late afternoon, going out visiting to practice my Tagalog. As I was the only man, I had no companion for those daily trips but had to go and make contacts on my own. With introductions given by Necy, who was still in Singapore, I had a list of people to visit. One was Efren, a young teenage student who took me to visit his home where I was introduced to *ube*. It is a species of yam (a tuber or root crop, *D. alata*). The tubers are vividly violet purple to bright lavender in color, which is grated and cooked. I was sitting on the stairs talking to Efren when this large plate of *ube* appeared. It seemed to be like a large mountain covering the whole plate. I was supplied with a spoon and encouraged to eat. I have never liked root crops much. I do not like swedes or turnips. Ube was much like these but coarser and for me hard to swallow. I looked at the family standing around me, watching me while I ate and smiled. Each mouthful was a struggle, but I was not going to offend anyone. I dug in with my spoon and kept eating. "I must not offend anyone," I thought, "I must keep eating." "I must be a good missionary." Eventually after much anguish I reached the last mouthful of that huge plateful of Ube. It was only some months later that someone told me that I did not have to finish such a large plate. If I had taken just a small amount that would have been okay. At the same time, they were surprised that I had not been given a small plate or saucer along with the spoon! Whenever I am offered *ube* now, I tell folk that I ate all I need many years ago in Calapan. Members of the church in Cubao all know not to offer me *ube*, or *ube*-colored things. Mind you,

Purple yam (ube) *Dioscorea alata*

they all do with many a giggle and laughter. I think everyone now knows the story of my first encounter with *ube*.

Brian Ellis with the attendees of a local Evangelical church in Calapan

My five months or so in Calapan went past without many events. I got to visit Necy's family and made friends with her married sisters. They all attended the local evangelical church where we missionaries attended on Sundays. My first sermon in Tagalog was delivered in that church if you can call it that. I prepared it with the language teacher, writing out the message in full. On the appointed day I just stood up and read the text in front of me. I had been studying Tagalog for just over six months. It is an easy language to start with not having tones like Chinese nor any difficult sounds. To speak it well, however, is difficult, and even after fifty years, I still make mistakes.

Along with the two new lady missionaries, Ann from England and Elvie from Canada, I attended the local church where Necy had grown up. It was an ecumenical church affiliated with the United Church of Christ of the Philippines (UCCP). The pastor nevertheless had evangelical leanings. Due to my limited Tagalog, I did not understand much of the service. After some time, I was asked to teach a teenage Sunday School class, and several of Necy's nieces were in my class.

My time in Calapan was spent in continuous language study with the late afternoons given over to the practice of Tagalog with those in the town who would be patient and give me the time. I was as green as they could be about language customs and the little things. I remember making friends with an older teenage young man. One day we went to the beach, and he took a fishing line with him and caught a small fish about five inches long which he threw on the ground under a coconut palm. The fish was still alive but would not be for long. For me it was far too small to eat so I quickly picked it up and threw it back into the sea. What had I done? That could be eaten, and any family would be glad of that little extra to their family's budget. I had so much to learn.

On the first occasion I went to this young man's home I was sitting on the stairs talking when they produced a large plate of "*ube*". This is the incident I described earlier. It was only later that I found out when back at the mission headquarters that I should not have eaten it all but just some—a spoonful, to be polite. Oh, I wish I had known that, as I did not like it one bit.

It was in Calapan when I had my first driving lesson. I had ridden a motorcycle in the U.K. and only once drove a van on an estate road for five minutes. That was all my driving experience. Cesar who was a medical doctor and to whom I was introduced by Necy through her letters, persuaded me to drive his jeep. This was an owner-type jeep like that used by the US military in Second World War. He produced a student license for me, and I drove around town sometimes with him, driving his jeep.

Towards the end of January, the time had come for me to move on to an active mission station. I was informed that I would be leaving Calapan and going to the western side of Mindoro Island, to the town of Mamburao where I would be assigned as a missionary. I would join Don and Valerie Byrne from Australia in their church-planting work in that small town. Occidental Mindoro in 1967 was one of the most backward and out of the way provinces in the Philippines. It was a fourth-class province the lowest class of them all.

MAMBURAO

Mamburao was the capital of the province, but it was isolated and a very small provincial town. The only way to reach Mamburao from other places was by plane or by a sea crossing from Batangas to Abra-de-ilog. Only a very small craft made that long trip.

There was a plane in those days which flew around the mountains to the Western side of Mindoro. It was an old DC-3 Dakota which flew from Calapan to Mamburao and cost just under £2.00 (US$3.00) for the fare. Both airstrips were grass runways.

At least I was able to fly from Calapan to Mamburao. Don Byrne met me, and I stayed at their home, with their family for over a year. We made the inevitable trip to the house with my boxes, which I had brought on the plane, this was by *calesa*. *Calesa*s were fast being replaced in those days by the motorized tricycle although you can still see a few around fifty years later in particular places. They were seeking to plant a church in this isolated place.

It was in Mamburao that I thanked the Lord that he gave me good deep sleep. He watched over me through an incident that took place in town. I had a room on the ground floor, and I regularly left my door open, which gave access to the small storage room and then to the kitchen. This also allowed more air to flow in my room. At night we would use mosquito nets because we had no screening on the windows against mosquitoes. Any way the house had too many open gaps under the eaves, which allowed air and insects to enter. I went to bed as usual, taking off my watch and putting it either under or at the side of my pillow, inside the mosquito net alongside my glasses. When I awoke in the morning my room was a mess. There were things all over the floor from my small wardrobe. Things from the table beside the bed were also on the floor. My watch was gone. A burglar that night had cut through the wooden bars in the kitchen and entered the house. My old ex-army shoulder bag was gone as was my binoculars, together with my hobby of bird watching. Nothing else seemed to have been taken and things like my tape recorder were left on the floor. It was later learned that someone had also broken in that night into a local policeman's house and stolen his revolver. The break-ins in fact, went on for almost a month, with the local police unable to catch up with whomever was responsible, and then stopped as suddenly as they began. Only small things, which could be easily carried, were stolen. I do thank God for giving me a deep sleep on such a night, as one never knows what will happen if one awakes to disturb a burglar, especially one who has stolen a gun!

STA CRUZ

Sta Cruz, was a small rural town and was about fifteen miles to the south of Mamburao. It would take me about an hour to travel by jeepney. The jeepney really dates from World War II with the vehicles left over after the war. These were converted into passenger vehicles. Since then, they have been greatly modified. They would have an entrance in the rear and passengers would sit along seats on either side. They are still widely used in the twenty-first Century, but now much longer and highly colorful.

The Overseas Missionary Fellowship (OMF) had a church planting work in this town, and I was requested to teach catechism classes in two different elementary schools as part of my language studies.

Initially, the first few visits I made to Santa Cruz were to visit the lady missionaries who were working there. However, as the work grew Leslie MacDonald, and his Canadian wife Lorraine replaced the ladies.

These overnight trips to Sta Cruz were my weekly routine where I stayed with Leslie and Lorraine. I had known Leslie from my school days. We've been at Southall Grammar School together in the same year. Neither of us had been Christians then. After leaving Grammar School, I met Leslie on a bus and found out that he was a Christian just as I now was. He preceded me to Bible School and then to OMF and the Philippines. When he moved to Sta Cruz, he had already completed one term of four years. He was now at the beginning of his second missionary term.

Leslie was to have much influence upon me in helping me to a better understanding of the truth of the gospel as he was a Reformed Baptist holding the doctrines of God's sovereign grace.

These weekly trips to Sta Cruz provided some different experiences of travel. I would wait for the return jeepney on Tuesday afternoon. There were only two or three trips a day. The vehicle would go around the few streets of the town blowing its horn indicating it might leave and I would dash out to get a good seat, preferably in the front seat next to the driver. It would not be so crowded as in the back. I was so happy that I often made the front seat as on two occasions we stopped and loaded a large cow into the vehicle, which was being taken to Mamburao for slaughter. It had its hooves tied together and then was pushed into the back with its feet in the air. The passengers would then climb into the long seats with their feet resting on the cow. The cow inevitably made its presence felt in several ways which we will not recount.

On another occasion, I missed the front seat and in fact missed all the seats. There seemed to be a good number of people travelling that afternoon. My only seat was on the bonnet (hood) of the jeepney. These jeepneys have all sorts of lights and ornaments on the front of the bonnet, which make good handholds. There were two of us on the bonnet and a number of men standing on the back of the jeepney holding on there. However, on this occasion, it was not just a matter of holding on. It began to rain and before long we were in the middle of a thunderstorm. I had an umbrella with me and tried my best to use it to protect myself from some of the lashing rain while hanging on and preventing the umbrella from turning inside out. I do recall giving little thought to whether through all this the driver could see where he was going. I was so happy when after about 10 minutes of this some passengers alighted from the jeepney, and I was given a seat inside the jeepney out of the rain.

A jampacked jeepney used to be a common sight in some rural areas in the Philippines.

CHAPTER 4

LOVE – HAS Its TWIST & TURNS

In the previous five months I had spent in Calapan the hometown of Necy, I had been able to get to know several of her sisters. I often visited them to practice my faltering Tagalog. Necy and I corresponded with each other as she was left in Singapore. Soon our frequent letters were noticed by the Lowland Superintended who also looked after the new missionaries.

As my time in Calapan and getting to know some of the members of Necy's family was ending, I found out that the Missionary Director in Calapan had known about my letters coming from Necy in Singapore. He was quite opposed to me writing to her and informed me anyway that we could never marry unless I was prepared to move from the Philippines to another country. Missionaries in OMF had to work in another country other than their own and Necy could not stay in the Philippines. He was not the only one opposed. Another older missionary from the American South was very much against such a thing. Two different races should not marry. It was wrong!

Under pressure and realizing that God had directed me to the Philippines, I must break off my relationship with Necy. I could only marry her unless I was willing, and she was willing to move to another country and begin language study all over again.

God seemed to be closing the door for us from East and West. We, therefore stopped writing to each other and ended our relationship.

GOD'S PROVIDENTIAL WAY

While in Mamburao, within my first few days there, something happened which was to change my life forever! Some would say it was a coincidence but there are no such things with God. Our heavenly Father is in control of all things. He was working His purposes in my life.

Don Byrne was talking with a visiting lady missionary Marylyn Smart, who worked in Calapan with students. They were discussing the mission's policy on inter-racial marriage. Particularly marriage between a Filipino and a Westerner. This had come about as since 1964 the OMF had opened the mission to Asians and others as well as Western missionaries. I overhead the discussion and was very surprised. The Mission policy of inter-racial marriage is - If a missionary lady was to marry a Filipino man, she would have to go with him to another country or leave the mission organization. The husband, being the leader of the family, had to be a missionary who would work in a country other than his own. This was OMF policy. However, a western man could marry a Filipina as he was already in a country other than his own and his wife then follows her husband. What I had previously been told had therefore been a mistake!

Having been in the Far East now for almost one year I was due for a holiday and had made a booking to go up to the Mission Guest Home in the cool northern mountains. In those days everyone went to the Baguio City up in the mountains of northern Luzon where at 4,000 feet the climate was much cooler. I therefore made arrangements with the OMF Home in Baguio City for my 3 weeks' holiday. I informed the Superintendent in Calapan of course. I was to leave in a few weeks' time via Manila.

After that, I received a letter from the Lowland Superintendent asking why I would be in Manila when Necy arrived from Singapore. He thought we had broken off our relationship, which we had. However, he still did not know the Mission policy accurately. Also, until that letter, I didn't know that Necy would be arriving from Singapore while I would be staying over in Manila on my way back from my holiday in the mountains.

The Lord was at work! We were going to be in Manila at the same time! She would also be staying at the OMF Mission Home in Manila at the exact same dates that I would also be staying there for two nights! Of course, such an event would be a fortunate accident in the eyes of the world. However, for a Christian, he knows that his Heavenly Father is in control of all things. It is called providence and in God's providence we were both booked in at the Manila Mission Home on the same days. It was like a bolt from the blue! The Lord was opening the way for Necy and I to be married.

Whilst in Manila we met and spent the whole day together at the Manila Zoo. That is the only time I have ever been to the zoo, and I do not remember anything about it, as we just sat and talked all the time. We could now get married! I did not have to leave the Philippines! The Lord's hand was on us directing and guiding us. To Him be all the glory!

We became engaged to be married! However, Necy was not a member of the OMF and had to become one, for us to get married. She had worked now for 16 years as a language teacher to all the missionaries and so was known by all. The Director, Cyril Weller who had been on furlough was now back in his position and Necy was accepted into the Mission but had to accomplish certain requirements. She had to go to Bible School and had to accomplish the best part of one year in such a school. She was therefore enrolled in the Far Eastern Bible Institute and Seminary (FEBIAS).

I would be allowed to travel to Manila once every three months to see her and only for two days. Well, it ended up more frequently than that in the goodness of the Lord. Particularly in the monsoon season (the wet season). I had to fly up to Manila from Mamburao by plane. The Mamburao airport was just a single grass strip, and it seemed every time I flew to Manila that when my two days were up the airport was closed due to the runway being waterlogged. On one occasion we got all the way to Mamburao and went back to Manila being unable to land and was raining hard, so the runway was not safe. That seemed to happen time and time again so that Necy and I gained an extra day or two when we could meet. Necy was studying temporarily at the FEBIAS College of Bible situated right next the Far East Broadcasting Company (FEBC), a Christian radio station beaming into many countries in the Far East and particularly China. We often met at the home of a missionary who was there. The FEBC compound was right next to FEBIAS with just a fence between them which had a gate connecting the two compounds. Very convenient for Necy and I. The Lord was so good to us, so often times we can get an extra evening together.

In the goodness of the Lord there were several other occasions too, such as the Annual Missionary Conference and a Sunday School Conference which increased the number of occasions we could meet.

PAMAMANHIKAN

One of the Philippine customs is the "pamamanhikan" (literally, to go up the stairs and enter a house, but now the idiom means "*to beg, entreat and agree on the marriage with the family*"). Normally the young man's family will take food to the home of his young lady and then the parents and extended family of both sides will agree on the marriage and make the arrangements for the wedding. My problem was that I had no family in the Philippines, and I hardly knew anything about the customs. I knew I should go and speak to Necy's parents and ask for her hand in marriage but that was all. One of my allowed visits to see her was therefore to be spent visiting her home in Calapan.

Mamburao and Calapan are on the same island of Mindoro but in those days, there was no direct way to travel from one side of the island to other due to the very high jungle covered mountain range directly down the center of the island. I could fly to Manila and then make the journey back to Batangas and then across by boat to Calapan. However, we had very little money and were saving all we could to pay for the wedding. One way which would be much cheaper was to get a boat from the town of Abra-de-Ilog in northern Occidental Mindoro across to Batangas on the island of Luzon and then take another boat back to Calapan in Oriental Mindoro.

19

I caught the afternoon jeepney to Abra-de-Ilog reaching the home of the missionary who worked out of that small town, in the late afternoon. I was then able to get to the pier to see if there was a boat available to get to Batangas. There was only a '*batel*', a large sailing barge leaving that night at midnight. Before midnight I returned to the pier walking the mile or so from the missionaries' home. A half-drunken man demanded I pay a fee to cross the pier to get to the *batel*. I was not going to pay without some kind of receipt but was persuaded by other passengers to pay or there could be trouble. You certainly must be careful dealing with half-drunks. I later found out there was a fee, and it was legitimate. As a foreigner in a strange land, and still with a limited amount of the language one often thinks people are going "to take you for a ride". Well, I certainly thought this half-drunk man was trying to do so not realizing that he was the official collector of the *arastre* (pier fee) imposed by the town government.

Just after midnight the *batel* eventually pulled out using its diesel engine into the mouth of the river and made for the open sea where it was able to hoist its large sail. The sea was flat and calm and looked like liquid glass. There was a bright full moon. The water rushed by the boat which glided along so smoothly under its sails. Suddenly like a torpedo there was this flash of light which glowed and left a glittering trail coming straight towards the bow of the boat. It seemed just to miss the bows. I hurried to the bow and clung to the rigging there to see again and again several dolphins playing with the sailing barge. What was so marvelous was the bioluminescence in the water so that as they zoomed towards the boat, they left this long trail of light behind them. One of the most beautiful sights I have ever seen. The Lord gives us extras, does He not? Here was I, full of trepidation on my way to ask Necy's parents for her hand in marriage. For a while in the beauty of that quiet ocean and the wonder of the dolphins playing with the barge, I was in another world and almost totally forgot my fears of what might lay ahead and how I would manage.

Towards the east in the direction, we were travelling there was a very bright red and orange glow in the sky. It looked like a great fire some way off. It lit up the sky at that point. It in fact was in Batangas Province and Taal Volcano which was in eruption at that time, and it stood out as a beacon for where we headed that is Batangas. Was this an omen to what I faced in Calapan when asking for Necy's hand? No, it was a beautiful spectacular sight an addition to the dolphins plays. After two hours of smooth sea, it changed to being very choppy and the diesel engine on the barge had to be brought into action as we made it through rougher seas to our destination off of the beach at Lemery. A journey of about 4 hours. We arrived sometime before 5 a.m. and I had to walk another mile or so, to get an early morning Jeepney to Batangas City and then another larger ship which would take me to Calapan.

The main Office and Mission Home of the OMF was in those days in Calapan on a small knoll overlooking the sea. After lunch and a nap, I fearfully made my way to Necy's home. No one volunteered to accompany me nor had anyone instructed me on the customs I should have followed. I was green as could be and had no idea what I had to do. A number of Necy's sisters were there as well as her mother and father whom I had come to speak to. If I had really known the custom, I would have gotten someone to come and do the talking for me. I should have also taken plenty of food with me to entertain the family. We live and learn! After some refreshment (not supplied by me I hasten to add) I asked the question I had come to ask. Could I marry their daughter Eunice. (Necy is her nick name, which everyone has in the Philippines.) Were they in agreement? Were they happy about it? Necy and her sisters were in the kitchen and kept peering around the open door and were in fits of laughter as I in my faltering Tagalog mixed with broken English was trying to ask for her hand in marriage. Necy and her sisters knew that the parents would never say directly that they were happy about the marriage. Who would be happy to lose their daughter? Filipinos just do not say that sort of thing on such occasions. If only I could return to the night before and the beauty of the dolphins, but I was here with the laughter from the kitchen and these dear old folks in front of me not saying anything. It seemed like ages before this came to an end. Necy rescued me from my predicament. Of course, they agreed but they would not say directly--this was the Philippines.

The Lord was so good and this poor stuttering, fearful Englishman was accepted to become part of the Goco family and clan. Necy was one of eleven children, plus a cousin who was adopted into the family because her parents died when she was very young, making them twelve. Here was I with no one in this world except my parents back in England. How different everything was. The ways of the Lord are past finding out. Yet He had his purposes for us, a Filipina, and an Englishman in this wonderful land of the Philippines.

CHAPTER 5

TOGETHER AS MISSIONARIES

Necy and I would be married in a matter of weeks, and we had been assigned to take up the work in Lubang Island based in the village of Tilik. My senior Australian missionary, Don Byrne, had been the first missionary assigned there and had visited various places in the small island chain which made up Lubang. Although he had labored there for several years, they had only seen one convert from the island of Ambil. After a gap of several years several single ladies had then been assigned to work there centered in the village of Tilik. Rosemary Sheriff, a member of Alexandra Road Congregational Church, in Hemel Hempstead had her first assignment there and she was to labor with two Filipina missionaries. One was a student who stayed for one year, the other was older and the experienced member of the team. After two years one lady had come to know Christ. We were on our way to visit her and to rent a house which would be the first home for Necy, and I. Don Byrne was to accompany me and would be making the arrangements for a house for us to live in.

GETTING SET UP

Don and I had left Mamburao in Occidental Mindoro at about 7:30 in the evening. The moon had hung like a beacon in the sky and the sea was like a mill pond. We were on our way to the island of Lubang. A journey probably of 6 or 7 hours. Mostly we would be running along the coast in sight of land until we got to the lighthouse at Cavite point and then we would turn out into the South China Sea to find Lubang Island. The boat was a typical small fishing boat, narrow and no more than about 3 feet wide by about 20-foot long. It was kept stable by two outriggers which consisted of bamboo poles lashed to stays about 5 feet from the side of the narrow craft. This would be our means of transport to Lubang.

It was a fine cool night for such a journey, and we were thankful that we had not tried to make it through the heat of the day. We made good times with the water skimming past the bow with a phosphorescent glow. In a couple of hours, we sighted the light house off our starboard bow. We would soon be in Lubang or so we thought. As we came round the headland the wind hit us like a sledgehammer. The seas rose and began to crash into our small boat. The boatman immediately had to slow the engine as we had to head into the waves. Water crashed into the boat, and I was wet to the core. Wave after wave came over the side and I pulled the small tarpaulin over my head as the men bailed wildly at the rear of the narrow boat.

The waves crashed into the small outrigger motorboat as the two boatmen bailed furiously. I crouched under a tarpaulin at the front as the waves constantly broke over the prow. We had no idea where we were, and we could hardly make any headway against the heavy seas. The moon which had given much light had now disappeared and everything was pitch black. Here we were way out from any land in a small motorboat, and we were at the mercy of the high seas which threatened to sink us any moment. No! We were not at the mercy of the high seas we were under the hand of our Almighty God who rules the wind and the waves. We were there according to His mercy. "Not a single shaft can hit, until the God of love sees fit."

We made very little headway and the moon which had lit our way slowly descended in the sky until it was no more. We were in the open sea and now everything was pitch black. There was no comforting shape of the land nearby. we were heading into the South China Sea. We had little idea where we were and which direction the waves and the current were taking us. We continued for hours slowly inching forward as the water continued to come in and men took it in turns to bail. Something like two in the morning we suddenly saw a light in the distance, and we began to make for it. The seas were not so rough so we must be approaching land. Suddenly through the dark, towards the light to which we had been traveling, we saw the white of foam just a few yards before the boat. It was a reef. The boatman quickly killed the engine and threw out his anchor. We ended up just off the reef. We could not see anything but the foam and the small light ahead of us. At least now the water was not coming into the boat as we were near land. Yet we were all cold and wet. We tried to doze as best we could as we waited for the morning. There we remained until the sky began to gain some light at about 5 am. The light quickly dominated the sky – it gets dark and light very quickly in the tropics. We could see the land and had an idea where we were. We were off the long island of Jolo in the Lubang chain. We turned West and made our way slowly along the coast. We were now sheltered by the land.

We were making for the channel between Jolo and Lubang proper. As we came into the channel the wind now became very fresh and we were once more battling with the waves. However, it was now light, and we could see where we were although we were still riding a roller coaster as the waves once more came over the side. We eventually arrived off the reef that crossed the lagoon where the village of Tilik is located. We made for the gap and entered the quiet waters of the lagoon. The trip had taken about 12 hours all together.

In Tilik, we soon arrived at the home of the Tria Family. We met Mely, the young mother of four who was a believer. We were hungry and downed some food before finding our way to a bed to get some sleep for a few hours before we went house hunting. We awoke in time for lunch and then had a wander around this compact village. Don did most of the talking as he inquired about houses and the possibility of renting one. We eventually learned of one that possibly would be suitable. It was owned by a young couple who were living there but they could do with the money and anyway they could always live with their parents. The large house in the third dirt street seemed suitable. It had a large downstairs room and two bedrooms and a living room upstairs. With an agreed rent of about £10 per month (over $20 in those days) we had a house. I now had to get some furniture and a wife.

We still had of course to return to Mamburao. Our small outrigger motorboat was all ready for the journey but neither Don nor I could look forward to another night of those waves. The Lord who had watched over us through an eventful night had other provisions for us. Tilik was the harbor for the whole island. Usually, one boat a week called in to pick up passengers and cargo bound for Manila. In the providence of God there was a Batel moored at the pier, and it was bound for Mamburao. In the six years we lived in Tilik I can only recall a very few rare occasions when a *batel* moored there. A *batel* is a large sailing barge something like the barges that used to ply the coastal waters of Britain. We were now able to secure passage on this much larger craft with which we could once again do battle with the waves that awaited us outside the lagoon. Most of these batels have a small diesel engine as well but they prefer to rely on the cheaper sail to drive them along. This time instead of running into the wind we would be running before it born along by the large sail. I stayed on deck all night as the smell in the hold with diesel fumes and the cargo was too much for me. We rolled and tossed in the waves and swell but made good heading with the strong wind at our backs. This was a much more pleasant way to travel.

I had been to Lubang and would be back again in about two months to bring my bride to the place where we would truly begin to be missionaries.

SETTLING IN

Upon our marriage on April 20th, 1968, we went to Baguio City for our honeymoon. It was a city popularized by Americans who wanted to escape the heat of the summer. The city of Baguio is located 5,000 feet high in the mountains of the northern Philippines. It was not a crowded place then, and we could get around

Mr. & Mrs. Brian Ellis
April 20, 1968

easily. We were able to enjoy our honeymoon in peace, enjoy the scenery, and enjoy each other's company. East and West together.

Our extended holiday, however, was to end, and we had to come down from the mountains and from our relaxation. We had been assigned to the Island of Lubang. I am never sure why, although I sometimes have a suspicion that we were a different couple. The first missionary couple in the Philippines of mixed race. Lubang was, as we were soon to find out, a very isolated place.

We had collected our things together which were packed in three or four boxes. These included the few books we possessed. We took them to the pier in Manila and looked to get a place on the wooden boat that was to travel to Tilik, Lubang. This was the Nuestra Señora de Loreto, a name we could never forget. We spent many an hour on that old tug. It was a wooden boat with folding army cots. That is if you could find a cot. That first experience was to teach us some things. There was no space. There was nowhere to sleep or even to sit. The boat was packed with a mass of bodies everywhere as well as the cargo they were loading. The trip by boat was at least 12 hours and there was no set time to set sail. What should we do?

In that first year there was still a plane going to Lubang. That ended shortly after we arrived there but the Philippine Airlines at that date still ran an air service to the town of Lubang and the grass air strip there. As there was no cot or even a seat for the night trip, we put our boxes on the boat and made a dash by taxi for the airport, having been informed that there was still time to try and catch the plane.

So, our first visit to Lubang was in luxury as we were able to get the plane to Lubang. There we boarded a jeepney for the 12 kilometers or so to the port village of Tilik in the center of the island, which was to become our home for the next 8 years.

Although Tilik was only a village, it was the center of the island because all the commerce passed through it because of the weekly boat from Manila. There were several shops in the center of the village which carried all sorts of things that one needed from fishing tackle, cans of sardines to shampoo. However, one had to pay a price. We soon found it was best for us to buy a bulk of supplies in Manila and have them shipped to us on the boat.

The house that Don Byrne and I managed to rent, a month before our wedding is a large house with two bedrooms and a large living room upstairs and a kitchen and a very large room downstairs. The door opened straight on to the road outside. The large room was to prove an ideal place to hold our worship services.

The only thing with the door opening straight onto the street was that the street was just a dirt road which was usually just a dust bowl, and the dust would then blow in the door and the downstairs windows. We kept the door and the windows open to let air in and some wind to try and keep cool. At that time there was no electricity or running water on the island in Tilik. We had to purchase a pressure lantern in Manila to have light in the house at night. There are no long evenings in the tropics. It gets dark about 6 pm, only varying by about one hour through the whole year.

Where we were to get our water? Well, there was "drinking water" from the river about a kilometer away. This had to be boiled. Yes, we did have a stove and we had shipped two tanks of gas from Manila on the boat. Initially as this was now the middle of May and the rains had not yet come, we used to get water from a neighbor's well. However, we wondered why we always felt sticky afterwards. We tasted the water and found it was salty. Tilik was right on the sea and the water in the well was salty. We were blessed in that house as the owner had installed a very large tank up near the roof which could catch the rainwater. We had to wait until the rains started which they did in June and then leave it a few weeks to really clean off the roof. We then could open the tank and fill it up. It was a large tank as I used to climb into to clean it and the opening was a couple of feet above my head. To get out I had to take a stool and climb on that hauling it out on a rope after me. Yet when the tank was clean and the roof had had time to clean, that tank of water lasted for our drinking water for the whole year! We did not boil it either.

CHAPTER 6

NUESTRA SEÑORA DE LORETO

Our first introduction to the Nuestra Señora de Loreto was a few days after our honeymoon in 1968. We were due to move to Tilik in the island of Lubang to begin our first missionary assignment. The means of travel with our possessions that were in three boxes was by ship. The only ship that went to Lubang was the old wooden Nuestra Señora de Loreto ("Our Lady of Loreto" – Loreto being a place in Italy where the home of Mary was supposedly miraculously transported from Nazareth.)

Once, a taxi driver took us to the pier in Manila to take the boat for Lubang. He expected us to go to one of the major piers, but our boat went from the breakwater, not the regular docking port. When he saw the boat he said, "That is not a ship that's a launch". Well, that is what the Nuestra Sera de Loreto was like. It had two decks where they placed old army cots for the passengers. Someone mentioned that there was an airplane. That is Philippine Airlines which was still running to Lubang. (They stopped their flights shortly after this.) Necy and I decided that even with the extra cost we would try the airport, as we had no cot on the boat and no seat at all. We therefore made a dash for the airport and reached it in time to get a seat of the plane, which was not full by any means. We arrived in Tilik after a 12-kilometre jeepney ride on rough roads from the airport.

The next morning, we awaited the arrival of the Nuestra Señora de Loreto as it was due in the morning after its 12-hour trip. There was no sign of the boat. However, it eventually limped in late that afternoon just as it was getting dark. It had taken over 24 hours from Manila as one of the engines had broken down. We thanked the Lord that in His providence we were unable to secure a cot and so we had taken the plane. We had had a good night's sleep and had time to begin to sort out some of the things we had with us in our cases well before the boat arrived. Twenty-Four hours was nothing to the Nuestra Señora de Loreto which often broke down, was delayed at the pier, or just took ages to arrive. Yet this ship was to become our regular means of transport when we needed to go to Manila.

The boat would make the journey from Manila once a week going on to Sablayan in Occidental Mindoro. It would then make its return trip to Manila via Tilik after three or four days. Necy got to know the captain well, as when the boat arrived going to Manila that was the one-day of the week when meat was available in Tilik. A cow and pigs would be slaughtered, as people would take fresh meat from the island to Manila where it cost twice as much. The boat would be filled with pieces of fresh meat hanging from the rafters for the trip to Manila. Necy would regularly meet the captain while she was waiting for the meat. He himself would be buying to take meat to Manila. This friendship with the captain was to prove somewhat helpful on one occasion.

We needed to make the trip to Manila, and we had packed our bag for the trip. I took our bag to the pier as soon as the boat came in from Sablayan. I wanted a good spot on the boat for the overnight trip. One problem with the Nuestra Señora de Loreto was the diesel smell. The smell and heat of the engines affected the whole boat inside the closed decks. Well, there was a spot at the rear of the boat where there were some cots in the open air. You took the risk of it raining but rain is fairly predictable in the Philippines and so it was a good spot. I claimed two of those old wooden and canvas cots and went home for the rest of the day. The boat spent most of the day at the pier before leaving for Manila late in the afternoon.

We heard the boats horn and collected the last of our things, locked up the house and made our way to the pier, which was only a few hundred yards from our house. When we got there, I was dismayed to see that the cots I had claimed were no longer there. The space where they had been being now occupied with about twenty large oil drums.

I groaned as we looked around the boat. There were now no vacant cots anywhere. I searched for our bags and found them on the roof where they had been thrown. I told Necy we could not go to Manila, as there was no where we could sit or rest. She said that we were prepared, and the house was locked up, we should continue even though we had no place in the boat. We would find surely somewhere after it got underway. Reluctantly I agreed to her request. She was the one who is very poor sailor. She then spoke to her friend the captain and he invited us up to the bridge. There we found two stools on one side of the bridge and squatted on these. It would be a long night.

Once we got out of the protection of the Tilik lagoon and from under the lee of the island the winds began to pick up and the old boat began to roll and toss for all she was worth. She was well known for this. Before long the spray came over the bows and hit us at the open window of the bridge. The windows had to be closed to keep out that spray. About 9:00 o'clock p.m., the captain asked if we had anywhere to sleep as everyone had begun to bed down for the night. We explained to him what had happened, and he asked if we had a *banig* (palm leaf mat), which we declared we had. He then showed us the space behind the man who held the wheel. It was about four and a half feet square on both sides, around two sides of which were some bunks. The bunks were occupied by crew members but there was enough space for us to fit into with my long legs doubled up. We put our mat down on the floor. Necy found she had a large jackfruit where her pillow should have been. She soon found out why her head hurt. A jackfruit had a many hard spikes on its thick skin.

Eventually, we began to settle down for the night to try and get some sleep in our new sleeping quarters. After a while Necy touched me and spoke to me. Something was touching her leg. She kept feeling it down the side of her. That was where the bunk was situated where the seaman was sleeping. The bunk was only about a foot above Necy. Was the seaman putting his hand down on my wife in the night? I told Necy to change places. I then settled down. Suddenly I felt it down the side of my leg. I would get this guy. I hit out as hard as I could with my fist and then up jumped this huge rat. It ran right over me and jumped into the other bunk behind our heads right on the sleeping man who was suddenly awakened. Drearily, he asked, "what was that?" "A rat", I squawked out. He was immediately awake and grabbed his shoe, which was in the bunk with him and began to beat everywhere he could with his shoe, but we never saw the rat again.

On another occasion we again had no cot but had to find a place on the stern at the rear of this small wooden ship. The only place was over one of the cargos holds but at least it was inside, and we would not get wet if it rained. Also, we could lay down on our reed mat we had with us, and we used some of our clothes in our bag for pillows. Again, the Nuestra Señora de Loreto was filled to bursting point. The place we had been able to fit in was slowly getting even fuller. As Necy and I laid down on the floor it was so crowded that someone at the other end had to put their feet up between us. We were literally packed like sardines. The diesel smell from the engines was very strong but that was not the only smell. The cargo-hold over which we were lying was filled with dried coconut (*copra*). This has a strong sickly oily smell, and it came up through the cracks in the boards. That was not the only pleasure, someone was taking a live chicken to Manila, which would probably be next days' dinner and it was tied up near our heads and of course would make a noise. The chicken's droppings were another hazard to avoid. We next found out that the door to the one toilet was just two people away on the other side of the sardine tin. We therefore had the pleasant smell of toilet along with the banging of the door every time someone made an exit or entrance. One experiences life in a different world on one of the small inter-island cargo vessels in the islands.

Necy has always hated sea travels as she is a poor sailor, but this was the only way on and off our island. We usually only left once a year if we would help it. We are thankful that we had arrived at our destination safely each time in the goodness of the Lord who watched over all our travels.

CHAPTER 7

THE MEN IN THE HILLS

When we arrived in Tilik in 1968 after our marriage we soon heard of the men in the hills. Lubang is generally hilly, and jungle covered apart from areas of rice paddy and the villages which are almost all along the coast or very near to the sea. There were all kinds of suggestions as to who these men were who often stole some of the harvested rice as well as tools and equipment used by the villagers in a number of the small barrios (villages).

Not long before, the son of the Postmaster had been killed by them. We also soon got to know Ka Sining who eventually began to attend our meetings. He had an artificial leg. One day he had been out away from the village on his own when he was shot in the leg, which was badly bleeding. He then heard these men approaching and so he pretended to be dead, and he had blood everywhere on him. He told me that he did not understand the language they were using but he just lay there pretending he was dead with his heart pounding within him. They took the things he had been carrying and left him.

He said he drank some of his own blood as he was so thirsty and eventually crawled away and survived. His leg however had to be amputated and so he had an artificial leg in its place.

Who were these men of the hills? There were many suggestions which we heard. Some thought they were NPA—that is, members of the New People's Army—the Communists which had been very active in central Luzon fighting the government. Others suggested that they were rustlers or smugglers. In fact, it was because of the activity of these men in the hills that a small detachment of the Philippine Constabulary was maintained in Tilik. From time to time, they were called out while we were there. Just to the north of the village there was a track which went to an old mine which was no longer being worked. However, there was some mining equipment and even dynamite stored there in a large safe. Therefore, an armed man was employed to guard the site.

One day this man came running into the village saying he had been shot at by some men. The police soon made their way from the village to the mine. The men were still there, and a firefight ensued. We could even hear the shots from the village. Eventually it stopped as it began to get dark. They had seen two men who as dusk settled, they were able to escape along a ditch. Night comes quickly in the tropics. The men had escaped. Again, the various suggestions of whom there was made.

It was such encounters that meant people lived in the village even during harvest time whereas normally because of stealing the harvest people would sleep in the field. They may have small huts out in their harvest fields, but no one would stay there over night because of "the men in the hills".

On October 19, 1972, it all changed. Many of the poorer villagers in Tilik often did not have rice paddies but grew hillside rice. This is rice which just relies on the rain during the wet monsoon season. It is much poorer in quality than paddy field rice, but it is still a good staple diet. At that time, we had a teenage girl who helped in the house doing cleaning and the laundry. We heard from her that her father's rice field had been set on fire. The detachment of the Philippines Police which was quartered only a few houses from us raced to go out to the fields to catch whoever was burning the rice. They came across the men and a firefight ensued.

One of the police told me what happened. They had been shooting at these men who shot back at them. He believed he had shot one of them and so he walked very slowly and carefully along this path and suddenly came upon this man sitting in the path. He said to him "*sumarenda ka, sumarenda ka*" "you surrender, you surrender". That is a mixture of English and Tagalog. The man sitting in the path however lifted up a large knife over his head which he was about to throw, so the policeman shot him dead.

Ka Sining

It was only when he approached the body that he began to realize who this man probably was. It was confirmed when he searched his trouser pockets and found a leaflet. This was not in English or Filipino but in Japanese. It was only then that they realized that all along these men of the hills were Japanese. Japanese stragglers of the Second World War which had ended in 1946 but which these men were still fighting in 1972, for the next twenty-six years!

A truck was called for and the body lay on the flat bed of the truck and brought into the village next to our house and the police detachment. It astonished everyone in the village to see the dead body of Kozuka, for that eventually became known to be his name. The dead body of a long lost Japanese solider who had still been fighting the Second World War. There was astonishment among the villagers but also anger. The Postmaster who had lost his son to these men took up stones and began to stone the body until he was pulled away by friends. I took a photo of the body lying on the truck.

Soon the whole village was inundated with Japanese reporters and TV crews. They seemed to be everywhere. Ka Sining and his tale of how he had been left for dead was soon discovered. Ka Sining used to attend our Lord's Day Worship Meeting every Sunday. A Japanese TV crew wanted to film him in the meeting. We made a sort of compromise. They could come in before the meeting began. We rented a small house for our church meetings and so the TV crew filled the place and started filming. Ka Sining came slowly climbing the stairs and coming and sitting down in the meeting. We then sang a hymn. The film crew were then asked to leave. Then we began the service properly.

I was also interviewed by another TV crew about what I knew and what had taken place in the village. It as a question-and-answer session. I suppose I appeared on a Japanese TV program somewhere. This was big news. The last soldiers of the Japanese Imperial Army who were still fighting the war. Onoda, following the death of his last companion, Kozuka, continued to live in the hills alone.

Who then was the man in the hills? They knew there was someone still there. Search parties were organized, loudspeakers were set up broadcasting messages in Japanese but to no avail, Lieutenant Onoda remained in the hills. At that stage no one knew who he was, but it later transpired that he had been training in Japan to conduct guerilla warfare behind enemy lines. There was an airstrip on Lubang from which the Japanese flew fighter planes. As the American invasion took place in the landings in Leyte Gulf, then Southern Mindoro and in the north in Lingayen Gulf. Onoda had been sent to gather men to continue the battle against the enemy. He therefore originally took several men with him into the hills.

Over the early part of his time there a number surrendered, and some died until there were only two of them left. That was when we arrived in Lubang Island.

Once it was known that those in the hills were Japanese several searches were made. However, in the end it was a young Japanese student who made the contact with Lieutenant Onoda the last Japanese straggler. This young man was Norio Suzuki. He talked with Onoda and was able to take photos of him. However, Onoda would not come out of the hills. He would only surrender at the command of his Superior Officer. He had been under the command of General Yokoyama, but Major Taniguchi was the one who had ordered him to proceed to Lubang. So, it was Major Taniguchi dressed up in his uniform who came to the meeting together with Suzuki. Major Taniguchi in his soldier's uniform delivered orally the command, the command from the Special Section of the Chief of Staff's Headquarters. Now Onoda was to leave Lubang.

Onoda was whisked away from Lubang as in many ways if any of those affected by his actions for the past 25 years had seen him, they might well have killed him. He and his companions had killed people, stolen, and destroyed crops and had caused fear among the inhabitants of the island.

Onoda returned to Japan a hero in many ways to the Japanese, but he could not settle there. It was so strange after his years in the jungle and hills of Lubang. He moved to Brazil where one of his brothers was and settled there. Eventually returning home to Japan where he died in a Tokyo hospital on 16th January 2014.

What strikes me is the utter dedication to duty, to serve his Emperor and follow the commands of his commanding officer whatever the cost. The Japanese looked upon their Emperor really as a god.

What of us who serve a far greater Master? Do we do it as faithfully as Lieutenant Onoda? Are we as dedicated to the service of our Lord as much as this man was? He served his god the Emperor of Japan with utter dedication and sacrifice, what of us? We have a far more gracious and loving Master yet surely our dedication fails so often with those of the world we can read of, like Onoda. Let us examine ourselves and ask if we would and do give ourselves completely to the service of the King of kings and of the Lord of lords.

CHAPTER 8

THINGS THAT GO BUMP IN THE NIGHT

What would we think of missionary hardship and such tropical problems with the missionaries 200 years ago in the 19th century? What people went through to serve Christ? What of our comfort today and everything we have? Yes, sickness and problems today but nothing compared with our forefathers.

One of the things that people think of when they think of the tropics is bugs, creepy crawlies, and more fearsome opponents such as snakes and things. We have however never been like the missionary in Malaysia who went to their outside toilet one day and looking up saw a king cobra curled up in the rafters above his head. No, we have seen snakes but have not yet had them in the house, for which we thank the Lord. We have, though, given battle with less daunting creatures.

My first battle was with a *tuko*. What is a *tuko*? It is the ugliest lizard you have ever seen with a great bulbous oversized head. They are over a foot long and if you want to know the sound, they make it is "tu-koh". Well, I had only been in the Philippines about a month or two and suddenly in the middle of the night there was this thunderous noise in my bedroom at 2:00 a.m. in the morning - "tu-koh". It was there right in the room and worse, this lizard had a hole right in the apex of the corner of the ceiling. The ceiling acted as a sounding board, and it sounded like he was using a loudspeaker to awaken me at 2 a.m.! Well, I recounted it next morning at breakfast and we all had a laugh. But this laughing matter did not go away. Almost night after night right in the middle of the night I was awakened by our friend. By this he was no longer my friend but a pest to be disposed of. How to achieve this? I had no idea! By the time I put the light on and jumped out of bed he pulled his head back into his hole. I had no means either of blocking this large hole in the corner of the ceiling.

Then one night just after I had put the light out there was a noise in the corner of the room. I quickly turned the light on and there was the *tuko*. He had come out of his hole and had chased a gecko (a small house lizard). He had caught his last meal I am afraid as I rushed across the room like a knight of old about to do battle grabbing one of my shoes in my hand. I let fly with my shoe and gave him such a thump he fell off the wall and his prey escaped his jaws. He fell on my chair. Now one of the things I have not told you about the *tuko* is that they have huge suction pads on their feet and this one-foot lizard can run across the ceiling as easily as you or I across the floor. Well, when he fell on my chair, he stuck to the hair which I quickly carried from the room and deposited outside the house. What happened to my *tuko*? I have no idea, whether he lived or died. He was a pest! Those *tuko*s are okay outside the house. In fact, in some way good to catch other things from the house but not in one's bedroom. My next encounter was with a dead scorpion. Or at least, I thought he was dead. We were sorting out some boxes in an old shed and there was this small wooden crate. We removed the things in it and there in the bottom was this squashed scorpion. As flat as a pancake. This was my first time to see a scorpion except on some visit to the London Zoo when I was a child. This one was a little disappointing. It was squashed and only about two inches long. I got a stick and poked the thing. It was not dead. This squashed pancake came to life. Up came his tail and he menaced all around him. At least this one was outside and not in the house. The previous junior missionary who had used the room was not using this particular house and found out more about scorpions than I wanted to know. He had picked up his towel which was on a hook on a wooden post and took a shower. When he went to dry his back, he had the stabbing pain of the scorpion's sting. It had been having a nice rest on his towel.

Many years later I had another encounter with a scorpion. This was when a package of tracts from the Scripture Gift Mission arrived. Now this package was rather dirty as it had been lost in the post office. The day of mailing was on this small package, and it had taken one and half years to get to us. When I opened it and it was partly open there were two small cockroaches and a scorpion inside. I do not think the latter were sent by the SGM.

Another visitor whom we often had was a little difficult to discover at first. We had some potted plants in our upstairs sitting room in Tilik. We began to discover each morning that the earth in the pots was pulled out onto the table. We put the earth back and the next day it was out on the table again. We eventually found out who was doing this as we heard him, and he began to run around our bedroom on a ledge just below the ceiling. It was a nice fat rat. Well, we took care of that one with some poison we were given by a friend in the village. All we heard was a bang of something falling down the stairs and there was our rat dead at the bottom.

On another occasion, one night. I saw this very large rat, and some of the rats we had seen seemed to be as big as cats. It was sitting on a ledge halfway up our stairs. Now I could not get at it as this ledge as it went in behind the stairs where there was a cupboard. There he sat. Well, some neighbors were talking outside, and I went out and asked if any of them had a spear gun. This was one of the means of fishing in our small fishing village. The men laughed when I mentioned the rat and I did not think they were going to help. I went back into the house and shone my flashlight on the rat still sitting on his ledge. (We had no electricity for much of our time in Tilik.) A few minutes later our neighbor appeared with his spear gun. I held the flashlight, and he took aim. The rat was about 10 feet away, but he was a goner. There was great amusement outside among the other men when they saw what he had speared.

Necy's main encounters in Tilik were with centipedes. Of course, we always had cockroaches and they are always a real pest. No matter what you do they always seem to come back. But the centipedes were another thing. These were up to about 9 inches long and they could sting very nastily. In our first house in Tilik we were always encountering centipedes particularly in the kitchen and of course that was Necy's domain. I would suddenly hear this scream from the kitchen while I was studying upstairs. I would rush downstairs to find Necy shaking and screaming as a large centipede would be crawling across her bare foot. In the house we only wore beach sandals. A piece of two-by-two lumber was kept handy to deal with such intruders. We did not like using sprays too much although sometimes we did, and we always had dead centipedes along with the cockroaches.

At nighttime we used a pressure lantern, but we always had to get inside our mosquito net. These pressure lanterns which were run on paraffin oil used a pump on the side to build up the pressure and to give a good light. The only problem was having to pump them so often and the heat they gave off. We would lay inside our mosquito net and read. It always gets dark between 5:30 and 6:30pm throughout the year in the tropics. The mosquito net was our only protection from the hordes of hungry mosquitoes that wanted us as their evening meal. But the light would bring many other insects which often would end up clinging to the outside of our mosquito net. A large six-inch praying mantis was always an interesting visitor as well as the large coconut beetles which would buzz around the light and bang into the wall.

Other visitors who we had regularly in all our homes in Tilik were bats. We had some that nested in the eves of our house, and they would often miss their homecoming and fly right in our open window and around our bedroom. They often went out quickly but sometimes did not and we would have a bat clinging to our mosquito net, sometimes only a few inches from our faces.

The Bible speaks of lizards even in the palaces of kings. *Proverbs 30:28 "The lizard you may grasp with the hands, yet it is in kings' palaces."* This would refer to the common Gecko which all our visitors are fascinated with. It is rare not to find one somewhere in the house. In Tilik for some time we had one which we easily recognized. He had a bent tail, and his name was George. We would find him upstairs but when we had our meals there, he would be skulking at the edge of the table waiting to see if there were any table scraps. He got to the stage that he would take something from the hand.

We also had larger lizards. There was the monitor lizard–the *bayawak*. Now, they can be three or four feet long or more and they can run fast. I had seen them climbing a coconut palm but my first encounter with one was when we had some chickens. When it was very hot, we would lay on the balcony of the very small house we rented at that time. We had a small chicken coop made of bamboo and thatched with palm leaves. One very hot lunch time, we were having forty winks (siesta) on the balcony when our few chickens began to make a big noise. I looked over the edge of the balcony and there on the roof of our hen house was this large monitor lizard. He was after our chickens. I again grabbed our handy *dos por dos* (two inches by two inches by about three feet wooden pole) and dashed down into the garden and was going to set about this chicken stealer. I never realized how fast they could run. It quickly got off the roof, and it ran for a hole in our fence as fast as any dog. It was then off up the street and disappeared into the front door of a neighbors' house. I never knew what happened after that.

On another occasion in a different larger house to which we had moved I again heard the scream of Necy from the kitchen. This time it was not a centipede but a *bayawak*. It had dashed in the front door and was under our refrigerator. By this time, we had a refrigerator which was run on liquefied petroleum gas (LPG), and it had quite a space under it. I called our neighbor, and he soon caught it with a piece of wire. He was going to have that *bayawak* for his evening meal. They are supposed to taste like chicken. Maybe because they have been eating chicken!

CHAPTER 9

FISHING FOR MEN

On the Lord's Day afternoon five of us walked to Vigo, the next village. It is about three kilometers along a dusty road past the Catholic Cemetery and then eventually past the Town Cemetery, through the coconut plantation and then on through a small village before we could turn off the main road to walk into the larger village of Vigo.

We had come to conduct our first evangelistic outreach in the village of Vigo. There were just two churches in this village of about 2,000 people – the Roman Catholic and the Philippine Independent Catholic Church (Aglipayan). Very much the same in idolatry and belief except the latter very rarely saw a priest and they did not practice oral confession. They had broken away from the Roman Catholic Church in 1898 at the time of the Philippine revolution against Spain yet had maintained all the trappings of Romanism.

That day we were to do our first giving out of tracts in the village. Four ladies from the small Tilik Evangelical Church accompanied me including Necy. As I was the odd one out, the only man, I went around the village and sought to engage some of the men in conversation who were sitting outside their houses talking with friends. The four ladies went off in twos to give out gospel tracts.

It was several hours later that Necy came to find me. She wanted me to visit a lady they had met in one of the homes. This was Lita Solis. Lita asked us a little about our religion and said she had been a Roman Catholic although was brought up in the Aglipayan Church (Independent Catholic), she had also tried the Crusaders of the Divine Church of Christ, a cult which believed that Jose Rizal, the Philippine national hero was a reincarnation of Christ. The Jehovah's Witness had also conducted a Bible study in her home for a while. There was a photographer based in Lubang town who was a Jehovah's Witnesses who would go with his wife and hold Bible Studies, but we had never heard of anyone joining the couple. Lita said she would be interested in having a Bible study led by the "*Protestante*" (Protestants). We therefore arranged to begin our Bible Study the next Lord's Day afternoon.

Members and attendees of the Tilik Evangelical Church

That was to be the first of almost six months of Bible Studies in which I took a series on the parables of our Lord and then later a series on the ten commandments. We would take one commandment each week. It was during this second series that Lita began to see something of her sin.

One Lord's Day afternoon we arrived at her home to be met by a very excited Lita. She cried out, "I have met the Lord, I have met the Lord!" She described how one night that week she had laid down on her sleeping mat but could not sleep. She began to pray and ask the Lord to show her that He was real and true. She said that she suddenly felt the presence of the Lord in that small room, it was awful as she felt his holiness and she knew she was a sinner. She could hardly breathe and was filled with fear, which suddenly lifted as she knew that her sins were forgiven for Christ's sake, and she said that then joy overwhelmed her.

She had told all her neighbors that Christ was alive and forgave sin. She had told everyone she had met what the Lord had done for her. There was a good crowd at our Bible Study that afternoon in that small home where Lita rejoiced in her Savior. We have seen Lita many years later when she has visited Manila, still going on with Christ whom she loves.

Moses lived in Tilik and his wife who was from that village had become a Protestant when she was a teenager in Manila. She had returned to the village with her husband and children. She attended the small church, and her husband would sometimes come. He was an excellent carpenter but men in the village did not like to work with him as he would work too fast, they said when he could have slowed down and make the work last longer. However, Moses was never out of work because the villagers liked the way he worked and the quality of his work.

His wife invited us to take a Bible Study in their home and Moses would attend regularly. It was after a lesson on the lost sheep of Luke 15 that I asked him where he was. Was he in the shepherd's fold or was he lost? He said he was lost. We talked with him some while and sought to point him to the Good Shepherd who laid down his life for the sheep. It was some weeks later that I saw him again and asked him how he was. He answered, "The Lord has found me." He had called on the Lord and asked him to forgive him his sins, and he knew they were forgiven. It was not too long before he was baptized and became a pillar in the church. The family later moved back to Manila where we heard he was continuing to follow Christ.

Shirley was a young girl in elementary school, about 10 years of age. She never missed Sunday School and came so regularly even though her parents were not believers. She began to borrow some pictures of Old Testament stories which we had and when we asked her why, she told us she was telling the stories to her classmates in school.

May is the great month of Santa Cruzan when children and adults dress up and parade around the town in honor of the Virgin Mary. Following the procession, a dance is held. This takes place every night. Shirley was chosen to represent the Virgin Mary in one of the processions, but she refused, she did not want to be involved in all the idolatry which went along with it. Even though she was beaten by her mother she still refused to take part in the religious procession.

When she was in First Year High School, she should have been top of her class as she was a very bright student. Yet she was not given that honor because she was a Protestant. She was constantly discriminated against in school because of her profession of Christ. Eventually her mother moved her to stay with her aunt in Manila to continue her studies. Her older sister Helen continued however to attend the church in Tilik and was eventually saved and baptized due to the testimony of Shirley. Eventually, Shirley became a doctor while Helen a nurse. Shirley came to see us in Manila when she was doing her practicum at a nearby government hospital. She continued to follow Christ and was in membership in a Bible-believing church.

Today some of those from Tilik now live in Manila and are members of a Reformed Baptist Church. We have members of one family, the Villas family in membership with Cubao Reformed Baptist Church. The Villas family were our next-door neighbors in Tilik where most of the family were converted.

We not only occasionally caught fish, but we saw in the goodness and mercy of Christ people coming to confess Jesus as their Lord and Savior and to rejoice in Him.

Men give much time and energy in order to fish for food. That surely should be a challenge to us all who are the Lord's people. It is not just pastors and evangelists who are called to be "fishers of men". Surely, we are all called to live a life of witness to others and to take every opportunity to make the good news of the gospel known to our friends, relatives and neighbors. What have we done with the blessed gospel of our Lord and Savior Jesus Christ?

One of the great problems in the Third World is that there is so much false and misleading teaching. We have all the teachings of the cults from the West as well as many home-grown cults. In the Philippines we have the cult known as the Iglesia ni Cristo (the Church of Christ). The founder of this cult claimed to be the Angel from the East of Revelation 7:2. They are a large cult claiming about 15 million adherents now here and have branches mainly among Filipinos in western countries. They deny the deity of Christ. There are other numerous cults which are just Filipino like a small cult that claims that the Filipino national hero, Jose Rizal was a reincarnation of Christ. Plus of course, Jehovah's Witnesses, and the Mormons. If you can name it, we probably have it.

Then of course we have many of the way-out charismatic groups. Large churches teaching "health and wealth" as well as the more usual Pentecostal and Charismatic churches.

The worst of American Arminianism (man-centered religion) is so common. I remember a missionary lady in the OMF coming back from an evangelistic training meeting in Manila to say, "with this method you can get anyone converted!" The so-called method was to get a person "to pray in the name of Jesus" and if they did so, "that person must have become a Christian". How terrible!

Rome claims something like 80% of the population, although today it may only be 70% and of course they could all do that, claim that is.

Years ago, when in Lubang we used to listen to the Christian Radio station news. This was the Far East Broadcasting Company. I can still remember the small "gospel snippet" that came in the middle of one news broadcast. "Jesus has done all He can to save you. He can do no more it is now up to you." That weak Jesus is not the Lord Jesus Christ of the Scriptures. The Lord Jesus Christ came into the world to save sinners and He saves them to the uttermost. The Lord said in John 6:37 "*All that the Father giveth me shall come to me; and him that cometh to me I will in no wise cast out.*"

The Apostle Paul writing to the Ephesians says Eph 1:3-6 *Blessed be the God and Father of our Lord Jesus Christ, who hath blessed us with all spiritual blessings in heavenly places in Christ: According as he hath chosen us in him before the foundation of the world, that we should be holy and without blame before him in love: Having predestinated us unto the adoption of children by Jesus Christ to himself, according to the good pleasure of his will, To the praise of the glory of his grace, wherein he hath made us accepted in the beloved.*

After their wedding, they went to Lubang Island, Occidental Mindoro to serve the Lord under the Overseas Missionary Fellowship (OMF) for about 8 years (1968-1976).

Again, in the second chapter. One of the most well know verses, Eph 2:8-*9 "For by grace are ye saved through faith; and that not of yourselves: it is the gift of God: not of works, lest any man should boast."*

We have nothing to boast about in our salvation. It is from first to last the sovereign, gracious work of our God and Savior. There is nothing we can boast about but simply praise and thank Him for His great love, mercy and grace. Our salvation from first to last is the work of our Heavenly Father. To Him be all the praise and the glory.

CHAPTER 10

AMADO DE LA TORRE

Amado was a simple man with a large family living on the island of Ambil, in the Philippines. This island stands out as it is really a high jungle-covered mountain which has a dormant volcano. There are many dormant volcanos in the Philippines and there are some which erupt regularly. One such dormant volcano was that of Mount Pinatubo which had been dormant for about 600 years as far as was known. It suddenly erupted in June 1991 causing much devastation and loss of life. We had about half an inch of ash on the roof of our house in Quezon City, Metro-Manila which would be about 60 miles from the volcano.

Amado lived on the far side of that island. He was a farmer but only had a very small area of rice field. Otherwise, he earned money by cutting trees on the mountain and sawing them into lumber for the construction of houses. He was a simple man with a large family.

On one occasion he was visiting an uncle on the main Lubang island from Ambil Island and found an old Tagalog Bible in his house. Amado asked if he could have it and so he began to read the Bible. He was a very slow reader, but he was reading the Bible. He had the Bible for a number of years. There was no one to teach him until something happened in the early 1960s. Don Byrne an Australian missionary with the Overseas Missionary Fellowship and a fellow single male missionary from Northern Island were assigned to begin mission work in the Lubang Islands. They had a small motorboat with outriggers and began to visit various villages in the islands. The roads were extremely poor and they would hold open-air meetings in the street. Well, they arrived in the village of Amado on Ambil Island. That village is on the far side of Ambil and can take several hours to reach there by motorboat.

The two men saw it was getting late. It gets dark early in the tropics and so they decided to stay the night in the village. They asked the head man where they could stay, and he showed them an empty house where they could sleep on the floor. It was while they were in that house that Amado appeared. He came to ask them questions about the Bible and what he had been reading. Don told me about that meeting. Amado kept asking questions and he kept them up all night asking about the Bible. That probably was the night that he was converted and became a true Christian.

We then met him some 5 or 6 years later and he hungered for the word of God. He would let us talk for hours. He was a very simple man, but he loved the Lord.

He was baptized and continued to live on his island with his family. We obtained a radio for him so he could listen to and learn from the Far East Broadcasting Company's Christian messages on that radio.

We visited Amado and his family on several occasions staying overnight in their home. That village was very poor. In Amado's home as in all the homes there were no toilets. You had to find a place usually at night in a certain vicinity or on the beach. There was no electricity, and all lighting was with candles or a paraffin lamp. We were used to paraffin lamps as we had no electricity in Tilik for many of the years we stayed there. Eventually electricity arrived in Tilik although we were often left in the dark by breakdowns in the diesel generator which was in the main village of Lubang.

There was an occasion when we invited a well-known Filipino radio preacher to visit us in Tilik for a Conference. We were able to contact Amado to inform him. The problem was there was no motorboat leaving for the main island so Amado borrowed a small outrigger canoe and paddled that canoe for over 6 hours so that he could come to the conference and hear the Word of God. He was a man who hungered for the word of God. He longed to know more and asked many questions. When he went home, he was able to find a motorboat going to his village, so they towed his small canoe behind and took him home.

Amado was a challenge to us. He longed to know more of God and His Word. What a challenge to people in the West who sometimes find it so hard to be early on a Lord's Day morning to their church meeting place. Some it seems by habit always arriving late. We have our cars and our comforts.

It does not take long to reach our place of worship, but it is Sunday and there is always the temptation to lay in bed a little longer and to get up late. Then what of the special occasions, do we really make an effort to be there? Do we have a hunger for the Word of God wanting to hear it proclaimed and expounded? Amado has always been a challenge to us who have it so easy in our cities and towns with our cars and means of transport. Let us ask ourselves, would we paddle a canoe for 6 hours across the open sea to be at a meeting for the exposition of God's Word?

CHAPTER 11

GOD'S TIME IS NOT OUR TIME - Agkawayan

In 1972 after we returned from a year's furlough in the UK, we were allocated money for a new four-wheel drive jeep to use on Lubang Island. This would mean that we could easily visit other villages which we had not been able to visit due to the very minimal public transport. The public transport only ran once a week when the ship that brought the various supplies needed for the island arrived. At other times you had to have your own transport or walk. Walking was out of the question going to the south of the island as it was very hilly, and it would take most of the day to reach the large village of Agkawayan. There were other villages closer, but transport was essential. The Lord, therefore, provided us with this four-wheel drive jeepney. It is ideal also for the monsoon season when the roads became muddy.

The four-wheel drive jeep for use on Lubang Island.

While we were in the UK the two ladies who had been posted to Tilik had been able to make a trip by jeep to the village of Agkawayan. They were encouraged by the people there whom they met and began a small meeting. So Agkawayan became an important location for us to visit. Our first trip there we did what we tended to do in the other villages we visited. We took with us a portable, battery run amplifier, loudspeaker, and microphone. Necy and I would sing some hymns and then I would read from the Scriptures and preach in the open air. While I preached Necy would gather the crowd of children that would always gather and take them aside to tell them a Bible story using a flannel graph board. What surprised us in Agkawayan was that some of the people had Bibles. We were invited to the home of Mang Juaning and we began to hold a regular meeting there. We asked about the Bibles and the story was told of how some Methodists from Manila had visited the village just before the Second World War and Japanese occupation. They had held street meetings and meetings for the children. They had also distributed Bibles to the children who gathered. This evangelistic venture ended with the outbreak of war.

Those who had Bibles in 1972 were the young people of 1940/41 these formerly were the young people that had received those Bible before the arrival of the Japanese. They had been reading their Bibles as they grew up and there were a number of them whose hearts were already prepared to hear the good news of the gospel. They were now in their 50s and the Lord now brought the gospel to them. They were the first converts and asked for Baptism. What a joy to see the hand of God at work in such a marvelous way. One of those people was Aling Lilay. She was the leader of the Aglipayan Church in the

One of the few pictures of Brian Ellis as a missionary in Lubang Island

village. She would lead the service each Sunday in the Aglipayan Church.

The Aglipayan denomination was a break-away from the Roman Catholic Church at the time of the Spanish-American war when the United States took over the Philippines and it became a colony of the United States. They would be in almost every respect like the Roman Catholic Church which dominates the religious scene in the Philippines except they do not hold "confession" and their priests are allowed to marry. Aling Lilay led the service in the Aglipayan Church every Sunday. There was no Aglipayan priest on the island, but one would usually visit about once a year. There were Aglipayan churches in most of the villages just as there were Roman Catholic Churches. The Roman Catholics did have a German priest in the town of Lubang who would visit the villages.

We began a Lord's Days service in the home of Mang Juaning. Although he was not to be with us long before the Lord took him home suddenly following our Lord's Day service. He went to lay down for a 'siesta' after lunch and never awoke in this life but in glory. We missed him so much. That service continued with Mang Tiago leading after the home call of Mang Juaning. Mang Tiago was asked previously to lead the service, but he could not speak at all in public, so Mang Juaning was the one who led the service, and I preached each Lord's Day. However, following that sudden death of Mang Juaning, lo and behold who was now leading the service? – Mang Tiago. His fear and anxiety all went away, and he was now able to speak in public and lead the service every Lord's Day. The Lord took away all that had been holding him back. We missed Mang Juaning greatly, but the Lord had other plans for him.

We had begun a Lord's Day's service in a number of villages. At 6:30 a.m., we would arrive by our jeep in Balikyas and hold a small service in the home of a lady who invited us in. Then at about 7:15 a.m., we would dash in the jeepney to the next village of Burol and hold a service there. Then we would travel the couple of kilometers to Agkawayan for their morning service. That would finish usually at about 10 o'clock or so. We then drove back to Tilik so that I could preach in the service. That service would have started being led by one of the men in the church. In the afternoon we would then go in the other direction to hold a service in the village of Vigo where again a small group of believers would meet.

What a blessed Lord's Day to be with the people of God and have the privilege of ministering His Word in these different villages. The Lord was at work calling out a people for Himself.

POSTSCRIPT

In 1976 we left Lubang never to return. We did hope to visit on one occasion but due to weather we did not continue. The reason we left is because whilst on furlough I decided I wanted to further the sovereign doctrines of our Lord and left OMF and joined Grace Baptist Mission to return to the Philippines still as missionaries but being able share *all* the counsel of God, not just some.

We were soon involved in church planting in Cubao, a suburb of Quezon City, part of Metro-Manila and the largest city in the Philippines. A very strategic place being a large commercial complex with hundreds of shops, entertainment center and one of the main hubs for provincial buses to all parts of the Philippines.

In God's wisdom, we had some families who had moved from Tilik to Manila, mainly because their children were now of college age, and they all relocated. Some of the first members of the Cubao Reformed Baptist Church were former members of the Tilik Evangelical Church. We still have some of those young people, now married and with their own families in membership with us in Cubao.

Yet another matter that thrilled our hearts was to hear about Agkawayan. A man from there had come to Manila and had attended the church of Pastor Manny Avena. Manny is a friend, and I conducted his wedding many years previously. The Valley View Church is a sovereign grace church. The folk in Agkawayan then asked Manny to help them. His church in Valley View to the east of Manila was able to help them support a pastor in Agkawayan. The village now has a Reformed Baptist Church holding the doctrines of God's sovereign grace. All praise be unto the Lord!

CHAPTER 12

CONVERSION and THE DOCTRINES OF GRACE

Being a missionary in a strange land should not stop one from searching the Scriptures and growing in one's knowledge of the truth. In fact, this is essential. Looking back over 50 years of missionary experience the first few years in the Philippines brought me to a settled conviction concerning the doctrines of God's sovereign grace.

I hesitate to say when I was truly converted and became a Christian. During my time at Grammar school, I began to go to a Methodist church. My mother's Aunt Maud lived close by my parents' home in Essex with her sisters. She used to go to the local Methodist church. That was why I went to the Methodists. I also had a dear friend at Grammar School, Anne, whose family were Christians, and she also went to church. Anne and I were monitors together for almost two years. I was about 16 years of age and we served out the lunches together on the table where we were assigned. We often had some free periods, and we would go out to the golf course which was nearby in the good weather and sit on the grass and talk for hours. I cannot remember what we talked about but I began to attend a church and so it was the Methodist Church.

"Copper" Clark the Physics master used to organize an annual school camp and I went every year. This particular year was at Ilfracombe in North Devon. The camp was only for boys, and we slept under canvas, dug latrines and cooked our own meals. It was great fun. I was now in the sixth form at school (Year 12). On Sundays we always went to church while at the camp. However, I now called myself a Methodist and so requested that I be allowed to attend the Methodist chapel in the village not far from our camp site. This was rather than the Parish Church where the other boys were going to church. Permission was granted and I went by myself. The chapel was packed as it was being used by a youth camp run by the Worldwide Evangelization Crusade (WEC), a missionary organization. They supplied the preacher. I cannot remember now anything about the message then, but it was one where an appeal was made for those "who wanted to be saved" to stay behind for counsel.

I stayed behind. I cannot recall much but I remember that I prayed and made a profession of faith. That evening I went to their camp site to attend their evening meeting and again was counseled. I considered myself a Christian but must admit I had great difficulty trying to read the Bible.

Leaving school, I went to the Borough Road College in Isleworth to train as a schoolteacher. In the providence of God, of which I am a firm believer having seen His hand at work again and again in so many marvelous ways, I was assigned by the college to "Digs" (lodgings) outside of the college but not far away. I walked there carrying my bags to find I had been assigned to the home of a widow, who regularly had students. There were four of us assigned to her home. One of the students had preceded me and he was already there. We got talking and agreed to share the upstairs room while the late comers would have to take the divided dining room behind a curtain which cut the room in half. We had the better deal being early. As we talked, I found that Peter Dye my roommate was a Christian. His family attended a "Plymouth Brethren assembly". Peter proved to be a good and faithful friend and helped me up to the end. Through him I joined the College Christian Union (CU) and became very active in the fellowship. We all met regularly for Bible study and prayer as well as inviting speakers for meetings, many designed to be evangelistic and so to reach out to our fellow students. Before long I found myself running the CU book table. It was the beginning of my great interest in Christian books. I had to keep it well stocked and often made trips to the Inter Varsity Press in London to acquire titles to sell from the book table.

At the end of my course at Boro, a number of us in the CU made a trip to the Keswick Convention, in the Lake District of Northwest England. This was an annual convention first begun in the late 19th century. It was primarily a holiness convention although it had begun to change a little in the 1960's. The meetings followed the usual pattern with the emphasis of taking holiness as an act of faith. We did not attend the afternoon meetings but went hiking and climbing instead. On a lovely afternoon our group set off to climb Mount Skidaw. However, I soon began to feel unwell and could not continue. I told my friends to go on without me. I laid on the grass at the side of the trail with a magnificent view below looking out over Derwent Water. I soon shut my eyes in the warmth of the morning sun,

I may have slept a little, but I remember at the same time much was going on in my mind about my life and my relationship with the Lord Jesus Christ. That afternoon may have been when I was truly converted because I know it made a great difference to me. I was a different person, and my main concern was now to serve the Lord Jesus Christ.

Graduating from college as a secondary school teacher, I applied to the Essex County Council for a teaching post and was assigned to Canvey Island Secondary School. Canvey Island is an island near the south end of the Thames Estuary on the east side.

I was living with my parents at the time in Laindon Essex, although after one year the property was possessed by the government for development of the new town of Basildon. My parents then moved away to Beccles in Suffolk, only staying there a year before moving on to Cromer in Norfolk and then to Glandford, near Holt where they remained until the end of their lives.

In Laindon I joined the local Methodist Church and became active in the church. Looking back, I do not believe the Pastor was converted, at least he held decided modernist views on the Scriptures and his messages were in no way evangelical. His wife sadly was certainly not converted. However, I was a willing young man in my early 20s and so they found plenty for me to do. One responsibility for which I thank the Lord was being asked to begin a youth fellowship on a Lord's Day evening. A small group of young people would meet together after the evening service, and we had many opportunities to discuss the Bible and the gospel. Sadly, I was still holding a very man-centered approach to the gospel, yet I believe some of those young people were truly converted by the grace of God.

An older married couple in the church approached me and asked me to begin a Bible Study and to lead a prayer meeting. There was no such thing in the church at that time. The church membership was about 100 but only 4 of us met each week for Bible Study and prayer. The older couple, a single older lady who had a Pentecostal background and me. This was a blessed time. It was during those two years in Laindon that I first began to preach, becoming a local preacher on trial in the Methodist circuit. I did not preach very often although I remember being invited to the local Baptist Church to preach in a youth meeting and they dangled a microphone right in my face with a large spool tape-recorder about 6 inches from my Bible. I was so nervous I am sure my message was terrible.

Yet it was in Laindon that the Lord began to show me that I had to make a choice. To be a good schoolteacher you have to really work at it. It is not just a matter of turning up and then teaching. A good teacher needs to prepare well, to think about the classes he is teaching and seek ways to make the subject interesting, understandable, and beneficial to the students. This takes time and needs thought and effort. Preparation should go into each class just as one prepares a Bible Study or a sermon. Yet I was becoming more and more involved in the work of the church and the teaching of the Word of God. A choice had to be made. Was my calling to be a schoolteacher? If it was, I should be a good teacher who would truly teach his students and be a help and encouragement to them in their teenage years.

As I thought and prayed about this, the more and more I came to the realization that my calling was not as a schoolteacher but as a teacher of the Word of God. I could not do both things well. At the same time, I had begun to be active in children's missions during the long summer holidays away from school. Through those holidays and the missionaries who were often invited to come along. These addressed the children that were gathered for the meetings. I began to form an interest in missions. Books now played an important part and I read all the books of Isobel Kuhn and other missionary stories. This progressed to actual attendance at conferences at the Swanwick Conference Center in Derbyshire run by the Overseas Missionary Fellowship. As those two years passed in Laindon it became clear that my future lay in missions, and I needed training in a school to become a missionary. My thoughts were then led to the Bible Training Institute in Glasgow, which had come into being as the result of the D. L. Moody meetings held in Scotland at the end of the 19th century.

My next step then was Glasgow. I had next to no money but began training in the old BTI building in Bothwell St, Glasgow. Those two years in Glasgow were very eventful. I made many mistakes and came to realize much more the sinfulness of my own heart and to know something of the humbling that causes being brought very low. I also was very much engaged in evangelism. The 150 or so students were divided into 4 teams working in various areas of the city. I was assigned to the Gorbals. That was one of the worst slums in Glasgow although it was slowly being cleared. The old buildings dating from the 19th century were damp and extremely dilapidated and many unfit for people to live in. I worked there for two years and all the time on the open-air team tramping the streets of the Gorbals on a Sunday afternoon, come rain, snow or shine; preaching on street corners and giving out tracts.

During that time, we also held a weeklong mission in one of the Presbyterian Churches. I was assigned to be one of the two student preachers. I can always remember this elder in the church who was very unhappy when we decided that we would not have an altar call at the end of the services. I was already beginning to question such thing as Biblical. We would invite anyone who wanted to know more about the way of salvation to attend an after meeting in a room in the basement area below the main chapel of the church. This elder said, we cannot do that, we would lose the atmosphere. What was "the atmosphere" that was necessary for a person to be converted? Was all this dependent upon some manipulation of men? Were we looking to the Holy Spirit to do his work in hearts or were we controlling the atmosphere and manipulating people?

During one of the term breaks when I would hitch-hike home to my parents in Glandford, Norfolk I made my way to one of my former classmates from Southall Grammar School who now lived in Leicester. He was married with a family. I stayed there the night and witnessed to him and led him through the 'sinner's prayer' as the means of evangelism. Yet later he never showed any real signs of conversion. An even worse scenario was when I attended a large Methodist Church in Glasgow on a Sunday evening. There was an after-church youth fellowship when one of my fellow Bible School students preached a gospel message and had an appeal. I counseled a young man in his late teens. We knelt down beside two chairs and again I led him through the usual Scripture verses and got him to pray the 'sinner's prayer' and ask Jesus into his heart. I then assured him he was now a Christian and his sins had been forgiven and taken away by Christ.

The next Sunday evening he was not at the church. I wondered where he was. The following Sunday he was also nowhere to be seen so I decided to go to his home. I knew his address and climbed the stairs up one of the Glasgow "closes". Usually, four or five floors of apartments off of a stair well. I knocked at the door and his older sister answered the door and I asked for her brother. She said he was not there as I saw over her shoulder that very brother diving out of the way behind a sofa so as to try and not be seen. He wanted nothing to do with me. Yet he had prayed the prayer! I had assured him from John 1:12 that he was now a child of God! What was wrong?

I applied to the Overseas Missionary Fellowship for service in the Far East and was accepted but because I had only been a member of a liberal Methodist Church, I was asked to gain experience in an evangelical church for a year. They assigned me to another Methodist Church in Plumstead, Southeast London. The only thing evangelical about the church was the minister who was a godly and beloved brother, Don Davies together with his wife Marion. Don told me on arrival in Plumstead that he was leaving Methodism when his contract with the church was finished. He could no longer stay in Methodism. I knew what he meant and found out even much more as I became his assistant in the church. There was a former Methodist deaconess who told me she was fed up with always hearing about the cross from the pulpit.

Then there was the local preacher, also a church member who in a sermon on Bible Sunday said that when you came to the Bible it is like panning for gold. You must swirl the water and mud around until the mud is washed out and you find a few grains of gold left. That is what you have to do with the Bible? Don Davies was leaving Methodism and so was I!

Don and Marion were wonderful friends whom I value so highly. (Don went to be with the Lord in 2013.) They were a tremendous help and encouragement to me in that year I spent in Plumstead and ever since. He began to introduce me to a different gospel, the gospel of Gods' sovereign grace. Don regularly attended the

Westminster Fellowship led by Dr. Martyn Lloyd-Jones. I read books which he recommended to me. I saw through the fallacies of Dispensationalism as a system of interpretation and understanding of the second coming of Christ. I had never been happy with the teaching as I had heard it all through my Brethren friend Peter, the person who was my roommate at Teachers' College.

However, it was not until I eventually arrived in the Philippines and was spending my time studying Tagalog in Mamburao in 1967 that the doctrines of God's Sovereign Grace became clear. I was not able to do very much, and most of the day was spent in language study with a teacher, books and trying to talk to children and neighbors in my very limited Tagalog. It was there that I wrote to the Banner of Truth Trust to purchase some of their books. I had been introduced to the Banner of Truth by Don in Plumstead. I sought to purchase a volume of Spurgeon's sermons as I wanted to see how Spurgeon applied the gospel. I also asked for a copy of the little booklet by Iain Murray, "The Invitation System". They also kindly sent me under their book fund the "Death of Death in the Death of Christ" by John Owen.

I do not recall being very affected by the introductory chapter of J. I. Packer to the "Death of Death". I read it and have read it again since. What I found so helpful however was Owen himself and his examination of the texts in the Scriptures dealing with the extent of the atonement. Owen is not easy to read but I devoured the book. Then I read that little booklet by Iain Murray, "The Invitation System". It is an examination of the system particularly used by the most renowned practitioner of the system that is Billy Graham. What I found so helpful was the second part of the booklet where he was speaking about theology. He said something which I do not think I had ever heard before. At least it had never registered in my thick head. Iain said that regeneration precedes conversion. Regeneration precedes faith in Christ. A person believes in Christ because of the work of the Holy Spirit in the miracle of the new birth. This is the glorious sovereignty of our gracious God.

I then was reading Paul's letter to the Ephesians, and it all made sense. Chapter one came alive, election, redemption all according to the riches of God's grace. "To the praise of the glory of his grace, wherein he hath made us accepted in the beloved. In whom we have redemption through his blood, the forgiveness of sins, according to the riches of his grace;" Eph 1:6-7. "I became a Calvinist!" Yes, if that is the term some people want to use, but I came into the liberty of the sons of God. I began to see something of the glory of our great God and Savior Jesus Christ.

That was why on our first furlough in 1971 we had prayed and sought a church where the glorious doctrines of sovereign grace were taught and loved. In the providence and goodness of God we were led to a small chapel situated amid some barley fields in Suffolk, Wattisham Baptist Chapel, where our godly family and friends in England dwell.

CHAPTER 13

NEW BEGINNING

In 1976 we returned to the UK for Furlough after leaving Lubang, never to return. We were back again to our Home Church at Wattisham in Suffolk. This time we were not staying in a caravan but able to move into a flat in Stowmarket which was owned by our friend and deacon, Sydney Rushbrook. It was ideal as it was on the first floor and one of the members of the church lived in the flat above us. We, of course had to spend time on deputation which we did for a while.

However, before going back to England, we resigned from the Overseas Missionary Fellowship because I had asked, "If it was possible if we returned to the Philippines with the Mission that we could use the 1689 Baptist Confession as the basis for our doctrinal statement in any church that we planted?" They told us that that would not be possible as not all the missionaries would agree to such a doctrinal statement. We could only have a general common evangelical doctrine which all the missionaries could accept.

I was extremely disappointed with this due to the fact that we had become convinced of the reformed doctrines as held by the Particular Baptists of the 17th Century. We were Calvinists in doctrine but also Particular Baptists. We wanted to plant churches holding the 1689 Baptist Confession. We therefore concluded that we had to resign from the Overseas Missionary Fellowship. The OMF is a fine Mission organization, but they have a very broad evangelical attitude to doctrine which embraces all shades and opinions. We therefore left with sadness the OMF.

We did not know what the future held. It was possible that I would become the pastor of a church in the UK. That however was not to be. Gordon Hawkins our pastor said to me. Brian, you speak Tagalog, you have lived and worked in the Philippines, you should return and plant a Reformed Baptist Church in that country. He contacted the Grace Baptist Mission and Frank Ellis who was with GBM came and talked with us, about the possibility of us returning to the Philippines under the auspices of GBM.

We began also to take some deputation meetings to acquaint churches of our new position. While on holiday and going up to Scotland we visited the Banner of Truth Trust in Edinburgh hoping to get some help with good books. We considered also starting a literature ministry in the Philippines as we planned to be based in Manila. At that stage the Banner of Truth were not able to help much. However, in the will of the Lord as we travelled back to Wattisham from Edinburgh we were in Yorkshire on the A1 and I knew that Evangelical Press had their warehouse in Ripon. So, we turned aside so that I could possibly find some cheap books to purchase in Ripon. Their warehouse was an old Methodist Church in the town. We entered and began to find some books. When I went to pay for them, I spent some time talking with Roger who was responsible for the warehouse and while talking with him Willis Metcalf who was on the Board of Evangelical Press came in. He heard that we were planning to return to the Philippines. He was most interested. Willis was a wealthy farmer but was using his money to prosper the work of Evangelical Press and the distribution of good God-honoring literature. He was most interested in our desire to return to the Philippines to begin a Reformed Baptist work.

Necy and I, after our visit to the warehouse, continued our long journey from Yorkshire back to Wattisham in Suffolk. We arrived in the late afternoon. About 9 o'clock we had a telephone call from Willis Metcalf to say that he and Bill Clark of Evangelical Press wanted to visit us. I asked him, "When?". He replied, "Now this evening!". They arrived about 11 o'clock and stayed to almost 3 a.m. We offered them a bed in the spare room, but they said they would return to Welwyn near London, and so off they went. They had come to visit us and encourage us to become representatives for Evangelical Press in the Philippines. I was eager to circulate reformed literature as it was books that had really helped me to an understanding of the Doctrines of God's Sovereign Grace. Therefore, when we returned to the Philippines we planned to work in Manila and particularly to distribute God-honoring books to the Christian book trade.

So, in 1977 we returned to the Philippines with the commission to begin a book distribution work, which we called Evangelical Outreach Inc (EOI). More about this later. We initially stayed with Necy's sister, Rachel in Project 4 in Quezon City, the largest city in Metro Manila or rather the Philippines. We then began to look for more permanent accommodation and so began to visit various areas where we were looking to rent a house. These we found through a newspaper. We tried different areas. One house we were interested in seemed fine. We asked how the water was and the owner said it was excellent and was always available. As we left, I decided to go and speak with the neighbors. She said the water was often weak and was a real problem as it was also not available at different hours. At another housBBane we looked at we asked about a jeepney line to the University area of Manila. This was because some young ladies from our church in Tilik would be staying with us to attend college. We were told there was a jeepney line in the next street which went to the University area. We said we would therefore take the house in Mandaluyong. As we left, I decided to check on the jeepney line. We went to the road where we were told there was a Jeepney line to the University Belt. We waited there for a jeepney, but none appeared. I then asked a passerby about the jeepneys. "Oh! There are no jeepneys here for a long while and none going to the University Belt". So, we cancelled that house.

We looked at some houses in Cubao, which is close to Project 4, but they were often not large enough or inadequate for our needs until we came to this bungalow in Miami Street not far from the Center of Cubao. It had a large living room and three bedrooms with a good expanse of garden. We decided to take it.

We moved in with our four young ladies from the church in Tilik whom we were helping go to college. That house has become our permanent home as the owner soon wanted to sell it and through the kindness of our church at Wattisham we were able to purchase it. It was ideal as it had some buildings at the end of the garden which were just what was needed for storing the books we were now going to sell in the bookstores in Manila and beyond. Evangelical Outreach was registered with the government and became our book distribution organization which continues still today and although we personally are not now directly involved in it. It is now run by our nephew and is located in a house on the opposite side of the road which is owned by our nephew and his wife.

We also began to look for a church in the area and heard of a small house church which was reformed in theology in San Juan which was a few miles away from Cubao. We had purchased a car from Necy's nephew and so we began to attend this "house church". Sometimes I was asked to preach in the church and was now taking an adult Bible study during the Sunday School hour prior to the morning service. Everything seemed fine. However, Christmas changed things. While taking the Adult Sunday School class on the Lord's Day morning I could not help overhearing what the children were singing in the Sunday School. It was "Rudolf the red-nosed Reindeer." "What were they doing?", I got intrigued.

We were also involved in a number of Bible Studies. One in Manila, another in a housing complex near Quezon City Hall, and yet another in Pasig in the home of a relative of the husband of Necy's niece. Well, as I was hearing Rudolf the Red Nosed Reindeer and realizing that the adult Sunday School class consisted mainly of foreign missionaries, I was so discouraged! Necy and I then began to discuss. "What should we be doing and what does the Lord have for us in this house church?"

Thus, the Lord moved us start our very own "house church" that will embrace only Reformed doctrines and biblical practices. We never came back to that church in San Juan where *Rudolf the red-nosed Reindeer* was sung instead of a psalm or a Christian hymn. Instead, Necy and I, plus four young ladies from Tilik began a work--right in our residence's living room in Cubao.

CHAPTER 14

CUBAO REFORMED BAPTIST CHURCH

As we looked around our own living room, we thought why not start a work in Cubao, in our large living room. We had the four young ladies from Tilik and we could invite others to attend. In fact, we then put a sign outside "Cubao Reformed Baptist Church". We also put a sign at each end of the street pointing to our house. We never asked permission and could never be able to do such a thing today, in those days' things were just done. However, it worked, and we had a few people after a while who began to turn up to see what this church was all about at 55 Miami Street.

Members of the CRBC "house church" pose for a picture in the sala of Ellis Residence in 55 Miami Street, Cubao. Front: Pastor Brian Ellis, Necy Goco Ellis, Frank Jamandre, Rolly Quen, and two visitors (not church members) Back: Edith Villas, Lolita Acosta, Jocelyn Tria, Ronnie Olivares, Cynthia De Lemos, and Jinatru Bautista

At the same time Necy and I did door to door visitation giving out gospel tracts and inviting folks to attend this new small house church. One of our first contacts was in a small squatter area in the next street to where we lived. There, we were invited into the tiny one room home of Mely Medenilla. Mely, by the grace of God, came to trust in the Lord Jesus Christ as her Savior and is a faithful member still today of Cubao Reformed Baptist Church (CRBC). She now lives in a different street with her granddaughter who also became a church member.

The church began then in our living room. George Capaque and our niece, Reby Bondad were responsible for contacts with students from the University Belt as they were both involved with the Inter Varsity Christian Fellowship. In one of the pictures similar to the one next page, Reby pointed some of the students she worked with to our home and this new "house church". Some of these "students" are still with us today such as Ramon Macapagal and his wife Bekha, Jess Villas and his wife Josie, Susan, and others whom we could name a few.

Cubao Reformed Baptist Church began to slowly grow, mainly with students from other universities, but it was growing. In fact, we rented the old house next to ours and some of the students stayed there. That property eventually came up for sale and so we with the help of our church in Wattisham made plans to purchase it. The owner made an appointment with me to meet her in Makati. I therefore made out a check for the money and made my trip to the restaurant where I was to meet her. When I arrived, she was already talking with a neighbor of ours who lived on the other side of our road. In fact, she had already sold the property to that person. I was flabbergasted and, in many ways, angry as we had an appointment, and all had been arranged. The next-door property was, however, already sold from under our feet. "What are we to do now?" I quietly whispered.

CRBC members pose for picture at the frontyard of the Ellis Residence in 55 Miami Street, Cubao

L to R: Ed Demo, Nonoy Rodillas, Tiburcio Eusebio, Susan San Juan, Marilyn Porciuncula, Dante Timonera, Rebecca Limbago, Norma Ignacio, Zeny Balatbat, Jane Rodriguez, Avin Castillo, Emilia de la Cruz, Edith Villas, Ramon Macapagal, Emma Sunogan, Marilyn, Betchie Lavares, Mana Arellano, Pastor Brian T. Ellis, Hector Koh, Joey Raneses, James Torrefranca, Nonoy Sornillo, Val Agron, Yolly Dote, and Susan Olivares.

Our nephew, Robertino "Bobot" Santos came up with a suggestion. He had been looking around and he had seen a vacant lot for sale in Harvard Street, across the other side of Aurora Boulevard. We went to look at the lot. It was quite low, and the rear of the lot had a pond where our nephew had caught a fish. The lot was for sale, and we had the money so, we purchased it. The Lord was directing us to this lot which was much better located than the one adjacent to our home. Our street has now become a main road from Quezon City Hall and is busy all day and night.

This lot in Harvard Street was in the part of the street which was a "dead end" like a cul-de-sac. There were no vehicles driving by except those that belonged to people living in that short closed-off road. It is a quiet street. It was also a close walking distance to the main shopping complex of Cubao. It was ideal! We purchased it, and then cleared the weeds and the pond and so began by building the ground floor of what would eventually become the Cubao Reformed Baptist Church building.

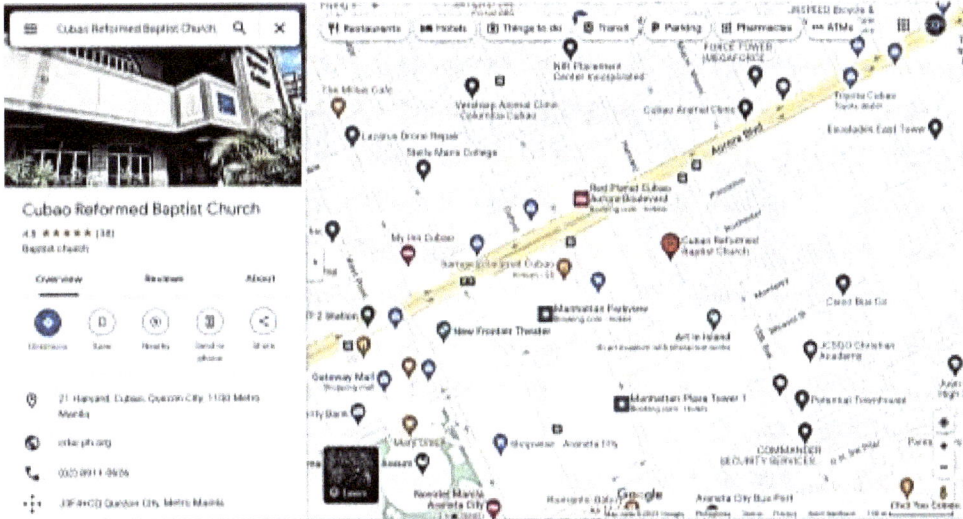

A few years later we were able to purchase two more lots next to ours where some old houses stood. Most were derelict and abandoned and so had to be destroyed but four were salvaged and then put to good use for our church office, student housing and home for Pastor Ismael Montejo's family. We now have three lots and a large complex where today we have even enlarged the actual church worship area so that we can accommodate up to about 600 people. Not that we have that many in our services except on special occasions. However, we normally have about 300 or more worshiping each Lord's Day.

The Cubao Reformed Baptist Church now, has four Elders: Ramon Macapagal, Ismael Montejo, Joseph Mangahas and me. I am beginning now, in 2019, taking a back seat due to my having reached the age of 80. The other Elders can carry on the work that has been going on all these years and we trust under God, will go on for many years to come to the glory of God and the benefit of the church here in the Philippines. Ramon Macapagal is now the senior pastor as I have basically retired having reached 80 years.

Group picture of CRBC members and attendees during its 38th Anniversary

Brian & Necy Ellis

Mon & Bekha Macapagal

Ismael Montejo family

Joseph & Sarah Mangahas

CHAPTER 15

AVENUES TO FISH FOR MORE MEN AND WOMEN

The ministry of Cubao Reformed Baptist Church has broadened. The Lord has given us more avenues to fish for more men and women to know the Lord. This is through our Literature work, Book and Tape Library, Bible School, Annual Pastors conference, work among the poor families and finally the drop-in-center for street people. These avenues have been a great help in bringing men to know the Lord and the doctrines of grace.

LITERATURE WORK

·EVANGELICAL OUTREACH, INC.

Returning to the beginnings, with the work begun now begun in our home (CRBC), various Bible studies that were being conducted, and through Evangelical Outreach Inc (EOI), which was the name we gave to our literature work. These books from EOI meant that otherwise Sovereign grace books would have not been available in the Philippines. EOI supplies books from Banner of Truth, Evangelical Press and other Christian Book Suppliers from UK and US to the local Philippine Christian Bookstores (PCBS) all over the Philippines. Through this literature work many have come to know the Lord and the doctrines of grace and one of the reasons for the growth of Reformed Baptist Churches in the Philippines. We were very busy indeed!

One of the men we first met was Rene Maramara, who was given the book, "Today's Gospel" by Walter Chantry bought by a friend from EOI. This was published by Banner of Truth Trust. We were selling books from the Banner of Truth and Evangelical Press. We used to put a small rubber stamp inside the back cover to say it was distributed by EOI. Through that literature work, Rene came into contact with us, then we began to have regular Bible studies in his home. He is now the pastor of a Sovereign Grace Church, which meets in Malate, situated in the heart of Manila, not far from famous tourist attraction, Manila Bay. I had the privilege of preaching at their church anniversary in 2018.

Another person who was greatly influenced by the literature which we were distributing to bookstores was Noel Espinosa. He picked up a couple of booklets written by A.W. Pink and published by Evangelical Press. These booklets were used to draw him to the "Reformed faith". He contacted us and over the years he has become a good friend. His wife Salvacion or "Bimbim" as she is called, used to be my secretary and I had the privilege of conducting their wedding ceremony. He is a very gifted man and is today the main lecturer and principal of Grace Ministerial Academy, a ministry of CRBC. He is a friend whom I highly value.

·PRINTING TRACTS, BOOKLETS & SUNDAY SCHOOL MATERIALS

Translation of materials into Tagalog like the 1689 Baptist Confession of Faith, became part of our printing ministry. Necy did a great job of translating, editing, writing most of the tracts, booklets such as *Pagbubulay* (Meditations), *Ang mga Walang Hanggang Katanungan: Batay sa Katekismo*" (Eternal Questions: Based on the Catechism), Lessons Learned from the Wicked Women of the Bible, *Ang Bautismo* (Baptism), Sunday School and Daily Vacation Bible School Materials for teachers to which some were printed in our small office. All these materials were used for evangelizing, tract giving, teacher's training not only by CRBC but also other churches who attended the annual pastors' conferences.

TRAINING MEN IN THE MINISTRY

·GRACE MINISTERIAL ACADEMY

Another ministry, that the Lord greatly blessed us to pioneer. It really started when I began to teach a few young men who wanted to study while the church was still at 55 Miami Street. Eventually, when we moved to the church building in Harvard Street, it began to grow and Pastor Noel Espinosa from Grace Baptist Church Los Baños

eventually did come to head up this ministry. It started off with about 5 students growing to about 20 students every year; these are mostly existing pastors of churches who want to learn and grow. Others are doing refresher courses.

Grace Ministerial Academy unofficially holds a lecture on Friday nights were all interested men and women can attend. But normally the

Graduates (front) and Faculty (back) of Grace Ministerial Academy in 2016

Bible school is only for males during the week, from Tuesday to Thursday. Long-term teachers included at various stages were Noel Espinosa (Principal), Rene Maramara, Joey Sarimento, Gilbert McAdam, Steve Hofmaier, Recman Denus, recently joined Joseph Mangahas, and myself.

I no longer teach but have retired from teaching Church History. Over the years we have had a good number of graduates of which many are now in the ministry in various parts of the country.

Another ministry which is connected to GMA is an extensive book library with over 5,000 books. This is a resource inside the CRBC premises and is available to Bible college students and others who desire to study more. It is of great assistance to people preparing sermons or lessons for pastors, teachers, lecturers, and other individuals who may not be able to afford to purchase many books. Recman Denus, who teaches Greek and Hebrew as Faculty of GMA, is the Librarian. (His wife, Debbie, used to regularly cook meals for the GMA staff and students.)

Recman & Debbie Denus

·PASTORS CONFERENCE

We hold a "Pastors' Conference for Men in the Ministry" every year since 1990. Most of the preachers were from England or the United States: Errol Hulse, J.P. Arthur, Jonathan Bayes, Tony Hutter, Jim Newheiser, Greg Nichols, Bob Carr, to name a few, as well as the Grace Ministerial Academy lecturers. Participants came from all over the Philippines. Each year, the attendance keeps increasing. Normally about 300 people attend.

The annual pastors conference deliberately began each time on a Tuesday so that pastors would speak at their churches on Sunday then travel to the conference, which could take up to 24 hours. Food and accommodation were

1990 - 1st Pastors' Conference

provided by CRBC. Usually, the conference would end on Thursday afternoon, and many would leave for home on Friday.

At every conference, free books were given out because of the book fund--books that helped spread God's doctrines of truth about a wide variety of topics.

Truly, the Lord made Grace Ministerial Academy and the Annual Pastors Conference to become one of the instruments to the growth and spread of many

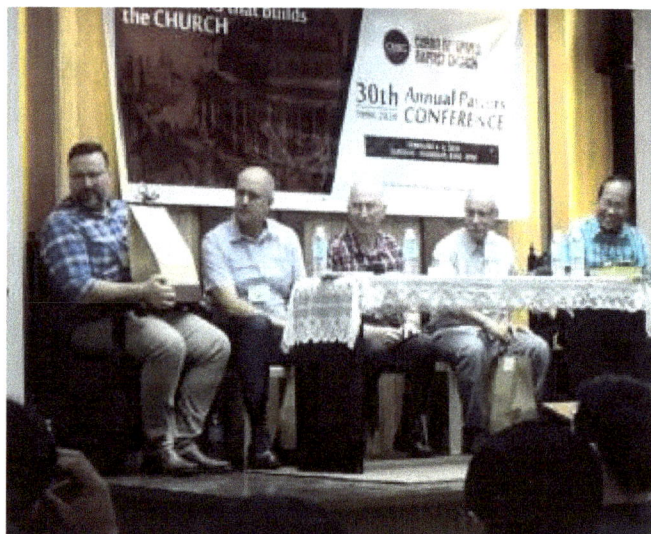

The Q & A Part of the 30th Annual Pastors Conference

Reformed Baptist churches all over the Philippines. Through this ministry that the passage was applied in Mark 1:17 "Then Jesus said to them, "Follow Me, and I will make you become fishers of men".

Another ministry which began almost from the start is the Tape Library. We had a tape library of sermons, such as Al Martin and Martin Lloyd Jones and the yearly conferences held at CRBC on various topics which were borrowed for two weeks which taught doctrine and practical applications of scriptures. Many of these tapes help initial contacts understand the doctrines of grace. Others are encouraged by them where they could still hear good sermons despite being in bad churches.

MINISTRY to the POOR

·Christian Compassion Ministries Foundation (CCM)

It all started because of an American church in Indiana who gave CRBC a large grant specifically to help poor and homeless. This ministry is through Christian Compassion Ministry (CCM) which the church registered by the Philippine Government Department of Social Welfare.

At the back of the CRBC building, it had four existing small flats. In 1995, one was converted into accommodation for girls headed up by three members and overseen by me. These members were Madelyn Salmorin and Maribeth Cano and Vita

Brian Ellis and his wife Necy with the CCM staff and clientele at the old CCM Office in Ermin Garcia Street. Circa 1996 Picture taken using an early cellphone camera.

Balaccua. They trained at Alay Pag-asa in Mandaluyong for 3 months for the work as housemothers and caretakers before they began the ministry. Arnel Carreon, a CRBC deacon then, became Director of CCM. Within a year, bigger accommodation was needed and CCM began the sponsorship of school needs and allowances for children. These consist of provision of school materials, uniforms, and hygiene kits. Over 250 families in the area are helped every year to keep their children going to school. At one time, we were having eleven Bible Studies in the area among such families.

CCM then rented a larger house nearby. This was when the children's home for girls started to become a reality. They needed an office for all the government requirements such as social/case studies, bookkeeping and other paper works.

By grace, CCM now has relatively earthquake-&-typhoon-proof buildings located some distance away: one in Masinag and one in La Colina, both in Antipolo City. These are for two separate homes, one for the girls in Masinag and the other for the boys in La Colina. The Girls' Home was finished in 2000, the Boys' Home in 2005. These are to help orphans or children who have come from difficult situations in their families. Some have been picked up off the streets.

CCM Girls' Home in Masinag, Antipolo City

ARTICLES OF INCORPORATION

OF

CHRISTIAN COMPASSION MINISTRIES FOUNDATION INC.

Name of Corporation

KNOW ALL MEN BY THESE PRESENTS :

The undersigned incorporators, all of legal and majority of whom are residents of the Philippines, have this day voluntarily agreed to form a non-stock non-profit corporation under the laws of the Republic of the Philippines.

AND WE HEREBY CERTIFY .

FIRST : That the name of the said Foundation shall be :

CHRISTIAN COMPASSION MINISTRIES FOUNDATION, INC.

SECOND : That the purpose or purposes for which such Foundation is incorporated are :

1. To improve and uplift the moral, physical, social, and spiritual life of abandoned and neglected children and that of indigent families without regard to their race, color, creed, religion, national origin, sex and physical condition, through the provision of residential homes for children; reconciling abandoned and neglected children to their families, providing educational assistance and training for street children indigent families and those needing help; and undertaking livelihood projects to improve the lot of those in desperate need.

2. To teach the children/or families about the love of the Lord Jesus Christ and to tell them of the glorious gospel of the only Saviour, Hope and light of the world. Such spiritual activity to be undertaken only under the auspices of the Cubao Reformed Baptist Church.

3. To pursue similar and supportive services as needed and necessary to attain the purpose of the foundation.

**First page of the Articles of Incorporation of the
Christian Compassion Ministries Foundation, Inc., drafted in 1995
for submission to the Securities and Exchange Commission (SEC)**

·DROP-IN CENTER

On Thursday nights we have the "Drop-in Center" which is for the homeless or street people. As many as two hundred gather to use our facilities to take a bath, have a shower and/or wash their clothes. They also can have a meal, often play games and above all, hear the preaching of the Word of God. A number of them return on the Lord's Day and attend the Tagalog Worship Service in the morning.

We have several who were formerly panhandlers but now in membership with us. They are, of course, no longer on the street but are now in much better circumstances.

This Drop-in Center gives these people dignity, to have clean clothes and bodies to still remain healthy. Once, we had a Christmas party for the panhandlers and prostitutes--not that we do believe in Christmas parties, but because they loved it and it truly made them feel human. That is, we could communicate with them, sharing the gospel to them in building friendships, and showing that we are all sinners, and we all need God's abounding grace.

Kuya Brian preaching in one of the Thursday Drop-In Meetings where the homeless or Street People are gathered

The Drop-in Center was adjourned because of the COVID-19 Pandemic. For close to three years (mid 2020 through early 2023) the national, as well as the local government restricted group meetings and gatherings to prevent the spread of the COVID-19 virus. Thus for 3 years, CRBC was not able to invite and provide for the homeless people around our vicinity. I was very glad to hear about the Drop-In Center resumption last June 15, 2023.

Deacon Virgo Ablao and a CCM staff Lowey Artaste are still the ones taking lead and new young men from CRBC take turns in preaching the gospel to them every Thursday as before.

Drop-In Center programs for the homeless resumed last June 15, 2023

CHAPTER 16

REFORMED BAPTIST CHURCHES OF THE PHILIPPINES

ANNUAL/BIANNUAL CAMPS

Another ministry not directly connected to me, or Cubao Reformed Baptist Church is the yearly Holy Week camping of Reformed Baptist churches. Held during the Holy Week because Manila seems to shut down for the week. Now, while the Roman Catholic tradition the week before Easter consists of parades of idols and mock crucifixions, the Reformed Baptist churches use the occasion for fellowship with the brethren of like precious faith (2Peter 1:1) in an out-of-town area.

A Reformed Baptist "camp" started to be held in 1981 just at the *sala* (the living room was turned into something where "campers" slept over) of the house in Miami Street. Indeed, the Reformed Baptist Camp a CRBC-hosted event until 1987 when Laguna churches hosted the Camp. The last Reformed Baptist Camp that CRBC continually hosted was held in Cavite in 1986. It should be noted however, that members from Pastors Rene Maramara's and Noel Espinosa's churches held parallel camps in the 1980s (although variably called retreats, brotherhood/sisterhood, familyhood, fraternal, etc.) before merging their Holy Week activities with that of CRBC. In the 2001 Camp, the idea of forming a Reformed Baptist Association of the Philippines (REBAP) by those holding the 1689 Baptist Confession of Faith, was brought up, and in 2002, REBAP LUZON was born.

Over the years the Reformed Baptist Camp participants grew so much in number that it became increasingly difficult to find a venue each year. Furthermore, we need enough lead time to reserve a place for us to fit over 400 people as there are now more than 20 Reformed Baptist Churches that gather for the camp for three days of preaching, fellowship, and relaxation.

Thus, because of the number of people and the sheer volume of resources involved, the Reformed Baptist Camp is now held just every other year.

1983 Reformed Baptist Camp

All these ministries have been a privilege for Necy and me to see what God has been doing in our lives and for us to have been a part of it. All the praise and the glory be unto our gracious Savior and Lord, the Lord Jesus Christ. AMEN!

RECOUNT & TESTIMONIES

MANNY AVENA
Pastor, Valley View Baptist Church, Cainta, Rizal

This is a short history of our ministerial encounter with the Ellis' in Lubang Island. Early in 2008, Valley View Baptist Church started praying for a startup ministry on local missions. After much prayer and seeking where to start, the Sales Family from Agkawayan who our church members had then informed us of a struggling gospel ministry in the Island of Lubang.

The ministry has been existing way back in late 60s and pioneered by a white missionary and his Filipina wife whom the Sales family did not know by name. The mission work we learned was also almost abandoned with a handful of believers struggling to survive in the absence of any gospel teaching ministry. Upon learning the situation, VVBC leaders paid a visit to the Island, and we found out, that existing work was lately taken over by a church planting group, ABCCOP, who after a few years also left the group without any leader to support the remaining believers. Owing to the facts of the isolated island, no minister could possibly survive the prevailing conditions of travelling back and forth. Travel was rigorously difficult because of the road conditions, and risky crossing of the sea. Only wooden boats ply the sea route to the Island and were known to be on a monthly duration only.

Manny & Ellen Avena

A single visit to the place revealed to us the very challenging nature of venturing into such a location. Ministry if ever to survive the challenge of the island must be with provision for a resident missionary. God in His goodness provided us with a person who is willing to stay in the Island with his family. VVBC sent Pastor Crisanto Miranda, the first missionary, in the locality in November 2008 to refresh the gospel initiatives and to put a strong presence of a gospel church in the area.

As we were going through the building up of the persisting brethren in the barangay, we learned that surviving believers know a certain Brian and Necy Ellis and they were with striking stories about the ministry of the couple in the Island. We got excited about it and relayed the information to Pastor Brian Ellis who was now in a local church in Cubao. Pastor Ellis was our officiating minister in our wedding in 1988. The writer was a student of the Cubao Reformed Baptist Institute during the early 80s and was for a time under the preaching and teaching ministry of the said Bible School. There were only two students on full time during that time. I was a fresh college graduate then and was still unassigned to a church, so I had the opportunity to attend all available classes of CRBI (Cubao Reformed Baptist Institute now Grace Ministerial Academy or GMA).

Pastor Ellis having learned our contacts with the community in Lubang narrated to us the history of the gospel ministry in the place which he commenced then when they were still missionaries of OMF. A surviving mother of a clan, 'Nanay Lilay', being 90 years old, learned that we know Pastor Ellis. She was overjoyed to hear that he was still in the Philippines and in the ministry. She narrated to us in her most vivid recollection how the couple ministered to them. There were five 'worship services' in the whole stretch of the island and the earliest starts in their place in Agkawayan at 5:00 in the morning. Pastor Ellis, from Tilik, where they were based (middle-upper of the Island about 30 kilometers up north--nearest the only port during that time), would travel to their homes that early and would start knocking at the doors for the believers to wake up to start their worship.

Another man by the name of Tiago, was a father to one of the believers. He was shot on top of a coconut tree by the Japanese World War II struggler, Hiroo Onoda. Tiago's son, Monching, is now a deacon in Agkawayan. Pastor Ellis had just left the Island in 1972, when the world-renowned Japanese Struggler surrendered to the Philippine Government, a fact of the history of the particular Island in 1974. Pastor Ellis was labouring for the gospel in loyalty to the Lord Jesus Christ, while Onoda was fighting as a struggler in loyalty to his country--a difference beyond imaginable comparison. Onoda loved his country; Pastor Brian Ellis loved the Lord and our countrymen, and he was willing to sacrifice his life for the cause of the gospel in ministering to that remote Island.

Another story of Sister 'Ebeng', now in her 50's was 'retrieved' 'binawi' in Tagalog by Pastor Ellis (brought back to her parents and to the church) after she eloped with an unbeliever. She was narrating to us her story in recollection which she cannot forget about the caring regard of Pastor Ellis way back when she was still young in her faith and in age. Now, it is part of her life-story, but part of a bigger story in the life of that ministry touched by Pastor Ellis in the place.

Today, the gospel of grace has spread to different localities through the influence of the ministry of Pastor Miranda. Reformation efforts are in the advance for churches which have lately sprouted in the island. These labours are felt and recognized in the entire Island of Lubang, owing this to the prior efforts of those who sow the gospel in the area.

I often cannot hold my emotions every time I thank Pastor Ellis either privately or in public because through him and his ministry I was exposed to the Reformed truths. The ministry which is under my oversight in the present is a living testimony of the fruits and labour of the person who gave himself to the Lord first, then to the Gospel ministry in the Philippines. Behind the man is a faithful wife whose ministry and exertion paved the way to broader avenues of services.

I thank them personally, with my family and as a church. To God alone be the glory for their lives and ministry.

RENE MARAMARA
Pastor, Sovereign Grace Church, Malate, Manila

The Lord saved me from a very dark background, but instead of bringing me to a good church to nurture me, the sovereign God, whose ways are different from man's ways, brought me to a very liberal church that was full of troubles. Looking back, I do now understand the wisdom in such a way, it made me hungry for genuine Christian experience. Also, because I could not find answers to many questions, it gave me much hunger for truth and guidance for spiritual walk. It was at this point that I received a gift from a member of CRBC--a book that enlightened me about true conversion.

Then in one IVCF (Inter-Varsity Christian Fellowship) camp that I participated in, with some members of CRBC, we were visited by a pastor whom they called "Kuya Brian". He visited just to see how his members were doing and also because he learned that the camp had a communion service, which for him, was against the rule of scriptures since the Lord's Supper is a church ordinance. Little did anyone know that this simple act was a ray of light to me a light that showed me what true pastoral care means.

Rene & Vangie Maramara

The only pastoral encounter I had ever seen at that time was seeing our pastor behind the pulpit, then disappearing as soon as the service was over. But observing Pastor Ellis that day, what I saw was a friend of the church members who was even addressed at times as "Kuya" and not "Pastor", which was a new picture of a pastor to me. Not that I am against the title "Pastor" but at that time, the title had created a not-so-friendly image in my mind. That was only the start.

My next encounter with pastor Ellis was when I learned that the book given to me, "Today's Gospel", was from EOI, which I also learned was part of Kuya Brian's ministry. Still hungry for knowledge, I visited their office warehouse in Miami St. at the back of their house. It was there that I met Pastor Ellis up close and learned more about him.

Now, I am certain that these were all part of God's plan preparing me for the ministry and Pastor Ellis played a big role in it. When growing in Reformed faith forced me to leave the church where I was an "associate" pastor, the only church I knew I could transfer to was CRBC, so I did. My only plan was to be in a good church, so I considered it already as a blessing that I was accepted into the membership. Pastor Ellis, however, saw a bigger picture, and proposed that I start an outreach in our place in Malate. I was very hesitant and resisted the idea. I was afraid to lead any Christian group because of my previous experiences. But Pastor Ellis insisted and persuaded me until we dealt compromise; I would gather the people, but he would do the entire ministry. As they say: "The rest is history".

We may think in our context that that was an ordinary course of church life: to begin an outreach whenever there is an opportunity. But we must consider that Pastor Ellis then was still struggling with some major reformation in his own church. He was still young in the movement and was a pastor of the only known Reformed Baptist Church in the Philippines. But his vision was big, and nothing could hinder him. Looking at the Movement now one will realize how much God has accomplished from that humble beginning. This can only make us truly say that God used Pastor Ellis mightily. May God get all the glory even as we recognize the man he used.

NOEL ESPINOSA
Pastor, Grace Baptist Church, Los Baños
Principal, Grace Ministerial Academy, Cubao

It was in 1982 when I first met Brian Thomas Ellis. I was a new and young pastor of a church which just covenanted in November of 1981. Already then, I had made steps of conscience which separated me from two previous affiliations.

The first was from a church characterized by decisions evangelism that was, and still is, the popular method, but about which I had read enough newly published books to discern its error. The second was from

Noel Espinosa with wife Bimbim (left) and son Jireh (right)

another church of Dispensationalist position. Having studied in a Bible college that taught Dispensationalism, I assumed that there was no other view worthy of consideration.

But again, it was some newly published literature that uncovered the wrong framework of that position. Both churches–instead of an amicable separation–chose to excommunicate me. I felt isolated and alone in my position. Meeting Brian Ellis was like knowing a kinship in a strange country. We proved to be of the same persuasion on many issues. It was a pleasant discovery that he was the man behind the published literature that I had been reading and was making such an impact on my life and ministry. This was through the work of Evangelical Outreach Incorporated–a distribution outlet for Reformed literature. Knowing him, not only obtained for me more books to read, but I also gained me a mentor. He was the senior to the young pastor that I was, and he made me realized that there were many more things for me to learn which also involved the challenge of unlearning old views I was still saddled with. Since then, I had been calling him "Pastor Ellis" – for that was how he became to me, though I never joined his church. He proved to be a gentle and wise pastor and mentor.

In the decade of the 1980's, Reformed Theology in the Philippines was treated with suspicion at best, with animosity more ordinarily. From a human standpoint, I would have crumbled had I not known that I was not alone holding that position. The company of Pastor Ellis became precious to me. It was a company that would be tested during that decade though. Was it the age discrepancy or the difference in personality? Could it be cultural difference between an Englishman and a Filipino, or perhaps, the usual tension between a foreign missionary and a local pastor? Pastor Ellis and I had our falling out every now and then.

But since both of us were invested in the interest of Reformed Baptist work in the country, by the grace of God, we managed to transcend the tension. In 1988, Pastor Ellis was instrumental to getting me a slot for study in London Theological Seminary. I spent a year of study in London Theological Seminary, with a lot of comprehensive extra studies outside the seminary. I count that period as one of the most productive to me intellectually and spiritually, and I have Pastor Ellis as one of those to thank for it. I returned to the Philippines, in many ways, a changed man and pastor.

Since 1990, Pastor Ellis and I have collaborated in an annual Pastors' Conference every February, and it went on every year. In 2023, we had our thirty-fourth year of conference. From very small beginnings, it was encouraging to see the growth to hundreds of men who are now in attendance.

In 1996, Pastor Ellis and I set out to begin our most major project together. It was the founding year of Grace Ministerial Academy (GMA). We agreed that its mandate would be: to train men to preach the Word of God and pastor the Church of Christ. We had help from other pastors at the beginning. But in the years following, we found the two of us left as the remaining main tutors. We thought that GMA might have to terminate. But by the grace of God, with dint of perseverance, GMA continued.

From the beginning, I was the Principal and Main Tutor while Pastor Ellis taught his first love as a subject–Christian History. He excelled in it and confirmed his vast reading. Countless numbers of men have gone through his course which ran many years, until his retirement from teaching in 2018. I have taken over the subject of Christian History since. I learned from him to teach it with the presupposition of the sovereign God of history.

We hold to the prophet's assertion: The LORD of hosts has sworn, saying, "Surely, as I have thought, so it shall come to pass, And as I have purposed, so it shall stand…" For the LORD of hosts has purposed, and who will annul it? His hand is stretched out, and who will turn it back? (Isaiah 14:24, 27).

Still, I discovered his shoes are big to fill in. I realized what sacrifice Pastor Ellis must have made to prepare lessons for his classes, the more I appreciated his ministry. Pastor Ellis is now in his much-deserved retirement. But he is still serving the Lord in other ways. I do miss my pastor and my mentor. I am sure that, by his godliness and wisdom, he has been used in many believers' lives. I know I am one of those. My prayer for Pastor Ellis, as that of the Apostle John for Gaius, is "that all may go well with you and that you may be in good health, as it goes well with your soul" (3 Jn. 1:2).

STEVE HOFMAIER
Former Pastor, Moonwalk Community Bible Church—Paranaque, Philippines
Pastor from 2018, Trinity Baptist Church, New Jersey, USA

I first met Pastor Ellis and Ate Necy around late1982 or early 1983. They were visiting our church in New Jersey, the Trinity Baptist Church, to give a missionary report on the work of the gospel in the Philippines. I was at that time teaching in the Trinity Ministerial Academy but very much interested in the cause of the gospel around the world. I was very much encouraged by the news of the many opportunities that existed and still exist in the islands of the Philippines. I arranged to meet with the Ellises in the home of Pastor Albert Martin, where they were staying during their visit. We spoke of the opportunities, the history of the work, as well as the dangers and difficulties. I had been to Africa for six months in 1981 so I was not a stranger to life in another part of the world. Their account of the work in Metro Manila interested me deeply.

Steve & Carol Hofmaier

As a result of this conversation, Pastor Ellis subsequently invited me to visit the Philippines in the summer of 1983. I was still single at the time, so it was not difficult for me to accept the invitation. I was there from the beginning of June through August 10 – leaving just eleven days before the assassination of Ninoy Aquino. During that time, Pastor Ellis arranged for me to visit a number of the churches in the country.

I had opportunity to preach in Cavite, Cebu, Cubao, Diliman, Los Baños, Malate, Ormoc, and San Pablo. I believe these were all the churches that would have identified themselves as "Reformed Baptist" at the time. I attended the first Reformed Baptist Pastors' Fraternal that was held at that time at 55 Miami Street. I was present for the covenanting of the Malate Reformed Baptist Church, now the Sovereign Grace Church.

Although the heat, humidity, pollution, traffic, and crowded conditions of Metro Manila were less than enticing (to say the least), the warmth of the people and the open doors for the gospel were more than enough to convince me in 10 weeks that I wanted to return to labor in the Philippines. On my return to the US in August, I proposed to my sweetheart, Carol, with the understanding that if she said yes, it meant joining me in going to the other side of the world from her home in New Jersey. You know the answer she gave!

So, we were married that November, and a year later, November 20, 1984, left our home for life in the Philippines. At that time, Pastor Ellis had been conducting a Bible Study in Moonwalk, Parañaque, in the home of Mr. and Mrs. Henry Seveses. They were the parents of Rolly Seveses, a member then of the church in Los Baños. Pastor Noel Espinosa had begun this evangelistic outreach, but due to the distance involved passed the leadership to Pastor Ellis.

When Carol and I came, after a week or so to get acclimated, the leadership was entrusted to me. The attenders of the study suffered with me as Carol and I were learning the language, and I began teaching more and more in Tagalog. The church in Cubao supplied men to help pass out invitations on Saturdays, going house to house through the housing subdivision. Several of the core attenders were from CRBC, including Rolly and Gels Seveses, Nonoy Sornillo, Yolly Dote, and Joey Ranieses. They all pitched in to invite friends and co-workers to join the Bible study. With God's blessing, the study grew in attendance to the point that we were ready to begin evening worship services after a year.

These were also owned of God with increasing interest and attendance, so that by April 1986 we were ready to begin a whole Lord's Day schedule of worship and study. This led to our covenanting as a church on June 20, 1987, with 22 founding members. We give all praise to our gracious God for what he did in planting MCBC. We as a church are deeply grateful to God for the help and ministry of Pastor Ellis and of CRBC, without which the Moonwalk Community Bible Church would not have come into being. May God continue to grant them strength to serve him, that they would prove true the promise in Psalm 92:12-15, *"The righteous man will flourish like the palm tree, He will grow like a cedar in Lebanon. Planted in the house of the LORD, They will flourish in the courts of our God. They will still yield fruit in old age; They shall be full of sap and very green, To declare that the LORD is upright; He is my rock, and there is no unrighteousness in Him."*

EDITH VILLAS-DANTES

I met Pastor Ellis at Tilik, Lubang Island in 1968. It was there that they were first assigned as missionaries. They were our neighbors and so I happened to attend a Sunday School they conducted.

Edith Villas-Dantes

After I graduated in High School, they took me to their care so that I could study in Manila. I resided with them at Miami, Cubao. Cynthia de Lemos and Jocelyn Tria preceded me who also came from our province, Lubang Island, and were part of the church that Pastor Ellis started.

It was in 55 Miami Street, Cubao that CRBC started. Cynthia, Jocelyn, and I were the ones teaching the children's Sunday School. We would pick up the children during Sunday mornings, around the area of the 15th Avenue, where sister Mely Medenilla, also among the senior members of the church, resided.

At one time, Pastor Ellis and Ate Necy brought us to a Bible Study in Pasig. On Saturday, we would arrange the chairs for the Sunday service. On some occasions, we would practice with Ate Reby Goco (sister of Ate Necy) for a special number. During Sundays, all would eat together, especially the young people, to have fellowship. The young people would have schedules for cooking rotation. There were many students then attending the church, coming from the Bible studies in campuses by IVCF.

LOLITA ACOSTA

I first met Pastor Ellis in connection at the church's work sometime in 1979, Ronnie Olivares, Jeanette Baustista, Jocelyn Tria and Edith Villas, handed me a tract, entitled, "*Gusto Mo Bang Maligtas? Hindi sa Kapahamakan o Aksidente Kundi sa Kasalanan*" (Do you want to be saved, Not from Accidents but from Sin).

Lolita Acosta

I was interested to know why so I looked for the

address #55 Miami Street, which is near the house of my elder sister Mely, where I was staying with at that moment. It was Sunday morning, so I heard Pastor Ellis preaching in Tagalog. "*Hindi lahat ng tumatawag sa akin ng Panginoon, Panginoon, ay maliligtas*" ("Not everyone that calls on me, Lord, Lord, will be save"), the Lord will answer "I do not know you". I thought the preaching is exactly for me.

Since I've been searching for the right way to know the Lord for my Salvation, the Lord touched my heart with His Holy Spirit. Until I joined the group to distribute tracts, we also fetch nearby children so they can attend Bible Study. I lived with the Ellises for 3 to 4 years. They sponsored my studies at NCBA, where I took two years Junior Secretariat Course. I worked in Evangelical Outreach Inc as a secretary. And after some time, I went abroad in Singapore. Pastor Ellis and Sansi (Necy) were concerned about my spiritual life that they even stopped over in Singapore so they can see me when they went to UK.

Pastor Ellis and Sansi (Necy) were widely used for the expansion of His Kingdom in the Philippines. Pastor Ellis was used by the Lord to lead the churches and start different ministerial works like the Christian Compassion Ministries Foundation, where children's studies are being sponsored by brethren abroad. Pastor Ellis is also passionate about Theology that he even taught in Grace Ministerial Academy for free. Soon there were also Bible Studies led by men like Arnel Careon and Rey Seveses on Fridays and Prayer Meetings were also held on Wednesdays. Sansi was also used by the Lord to initiate ministries like Sunday School for kids. They also have Daily Vacation Bible School every school vacation where children come to attend and learn the Bible. She also passionately trained the ladies spiritually and led various ladies' studies. Providence took me to the province to take care of my sickly mother, but Pastor Ellis and Sansi still remember and pray for me. I moved to a local church there but whenever I come here in Quezon City, I always visit and feel welcome by the fellow believers in Cubao Reformed Baptist Church.

EMELIA MEDENILLA (Mely)

I am Emilia Medenilla, known by everyone as "Ate Mely". The Lord used my younger sister Lolit as an instrument so Pastor Ellis can start a Bible Study near our area. That was when I first met Pastor Ellis.

Mely Medenilla

We used to live in the slums and every time Pastor Ellis came for our Bible Study, he sometimes would hit his head on the roof of our house because he is so tall. I remember that I don't like attending his Bible Studies.

I would prefer to focus on my work as a dress maker so I can provide for my family's needs. I even asked my son to lie and tell Pastor Ellis and the Bible Study Leaders that I'm not at home, so I don't have to attend his Bible Studies. My son said, "My mother said, she is not at home." I was so embarrassed!

Since then, I attended the Bible Studies, and the Lord opened my heart to His Word. I learned that I don't have to worry for my everyday needs because the Lord will provide for them.

I became a member of Cubao Reformed Baptist Church, and I also brought my children to the church. Pastor Ellis and Ate Necy became my advisers. They always counsel me every time I have fight with my husband who was a drunkard and unbeliever back then. They encouraged me to be active in the church until now that I am 75 years old. I still strive to pray every day that the Lord will keep me until the end.

Praise God for their lives and even the diligent men whom God called to the ministry of many souls like me today.

MARIBETTE CANO-EVANS

Pastor Ellis or Tito Brian, to which I and many others liked to call him, has so many remarkable characteristics that I could admire and remember in my entire life. He is the person that you would really admire, not because he is British or *Puti* (a Filipino tag for Caucasians), but because of his characteristics as a person. Of course, with the help of his loveliest wife Ate Necy, whom God has given to be with him during his journey on earth. She contributed a lot in Pastor Brian Ellis' accomplishments in his earthly ministry for God's kingdom.

Maribette

I became a Christian in October in 1986 in Novaliches, QC, before I met Tito Brian. I went back home to Bicol Region in 1987. My neighbor in Bicol (from Lumban, Laguna) asked me if I wanted to work in Lumban. So, I went there. I was praying to God constantly to bring me to a church with true believers. Providentially, God brought me there and worked first for Ate Mila (a member of Puritan Reformed Baptist Church). So Ate Mila would always ask me to attend with them on Sundays. I became a member there eventually in 1987. Pastor Arnel Cajayon our pastor, gave me a chance to teach in the Sunday school for children. Thanks to God I was able to finish High School and first year college there in Lumban.

While in Lumban, I came to know Pastor Ellis and Ate Necy because Pastor Arnel Cajayon was one of the earliest students of Pastor Ellis at the Bible school at 55 Miami Street, Cubao. This couple is known to many churches since Pastor Ellis helped establish many Reformed Baptist Churches in the Philippines.

In 1991, I went abroad and worked there for 2 years. When I went home to the Philippines in 1993, Pastor Cajayon helped me to seek God's will in Manila. He suggested that I should go to Pastor Ellis at 55 Miami (where I stayed for a long while). I also transferred my membership to CRBC. This couple would always see my potentials; they helped me a lot in so many ways. They treated me like their own daughter. Ate Necy taught me to be a good homemaker.

While studying in College, Pastor Ellis and Ate Necy asked me to teach Sunday School for children and do some office jobs like helping Ate Necy translate some devotional materials, hymns, and Sunday School Materials to Tagalog. Pastor Ellis, together with the church, decided to start Christian Compassion Ministries (CCM) in 1995. Pastor Ellis sent me and 2 other CRBC ladies, Madeline Salmorin and Ate Vita Balaccua to undergo training at Alay Pag-Asa in Mandaluyong.

After 3 months of training, we started the ministry of CCM in the apartment at the back of CRBC building. We performed all types of duties there, like that of social workers, house parents, tutors, street educator and community workers because the organizational structure of CCM was not that explicit yet because the ministry was new for us.

This couple has lots of contributions of who I am now. During the pandemic, I had a chance to visit Pastor Ellis and Ate Necy in their house in Miami Street in Cubao. Indeed I missed this lovely couple. Ate Necy whispered to me, "Beth, please help in finalizing Pastor Ellis' biography".

I would like to thank Pastor Ellis and Ate Necy for their great contributions to God's Kingdom on Earth, especially to me personally. Thank you, Pastor Ellis, for making me part of your family on earth. See you in Heavenly Kingdom where God reigns and Jesus Christ sits at right hand of the Father.

MADELYN SALMORIN-BARRIENTO

I met Pastor Brian Ellis and *Ate* Necy through my friend Jeanette Bautista-Olivares who invited me to attend an evening service in 1979. I was 14 years old then. I came with my sister Susanita Salmorin who was first to become a member of Cubao Reformed Baptist Church. Eventually, I joined the church and remained so since then. When the CRBC was in its infancy, we would usually join in the efforts to evangelize the community during Sunday early afternoons.

Israel & Madeline Barriento

Pastor Ellis would preach in the various streets of Cubao while we would be handing out tracts to people. Passers-by would usually stop and get amazed at the sight of a white man speaking in Tagalog fluently. Pastor Ellis would even go through the slum areas where he would have to walk carefully and slowly, crossing unstable man-made bridges that can hardly carry his weight. After the open-air meetings, we would usually return to the Ellis' living room for an evening service.

A little later during this period, a Bible study was also conducted in Moonwalk at the house of Tita Seveses. We would visit what would become the Moonwalk Community Bible Church after we take our lunch and then return for the evening service.

There were times that we would even sleep over at the Ellis' during Sundays. Every Sunday morning, Ate Necy, Edith, and Joselyn would teach the children's Sunday school. Ate Necy would prepare snacks for kids before the English service starts at 10:00 am and end by 12:00 noon. We would then take our lunch together after the church service.

The church gradually grew, and we had an outing at the Luneta Park once. I remember Ate Necy asking what food I have packed. I answered that I brought a loaf of bread. She asked that we share it together. I didn't want to because I preferred to keep it to myself. Sister Necy was laughing at me. My loaf of bread doesn't even come with any spread.

Ate Necy was a tremendous help in ministering to the church. She led the ladies Bible studies and taught them how to cook. They would prepare and cook first then as the food are cooking then they would have their Bible Study. This was held every Wednesday. She mentored ladies how to make Sunday School lessons and how to teach Sunday School children not just in CRBC but in other sister churches as well.

We thank the Lord who used Pastor Ellis to minister in the Philippines. I am among the beneficiaries of his ministries. Pastor Ellis also started a ministry to help children from the streets. He wanted to see them educated and provided for. This became the Christian Compassion Ministries Foundation Inc.. It started with three staff which included me, Vita Balaccua, and Maribeth Cano. As Ate Necy said, the Enemy will actively seek the ruin of the Lord's work. Pastor Ellis and sister Necy were only instruments. Praise is due to God and not unto men. May the cause of the Reformation in the Philippines endure to the end.

SARAH TOWNSEND
daughter of Pastor Gordon Hawkins

Mr. and Mrs. Brian Ellis were originally missionaries with OMF but driven to leave due to a wide divergence of beliefs and through reading the Banner of Truth magazine came powerfully and irrevocably to the Doctrines of free and sovereign grace. They were recommended by Erroll Hulse from the Banner of Truth to visit Wattisham Baptist Church (WBC) where Gordon Hawkins was a pastor. In 1971, this is what they did and on desiring baptism, Gordon Hawkins officiated. They then became members and the whole church loved them and endeared themselves to each other. Rev. Gordon Hawkins strongly advised them to return to the Philippines even though Pastor Brian's parents lived in the UK not far from Wattisham. This they did–heading back and this time to Manila. Setting up a book work with the help of Evangelical Press–wholesaling God-honouring Christian books. Soon a group of people began meeting for a worship service in their home each Lord's Day. In 1979, a small church covenanted together formally. The house in Miami Street was purchased with money from Wattisham Baptist Church and other churches in UK. In 1996, an academy for training of ministries was convened. Pastor and Mrs. Ellis returned on furlough to WBC regularly and was always a joy for them.

On returning to the UK and Wattisham on furlough every 2-3 years–the church organized welcome tea, and service and every face was happy and beaming, with the sheer delight of having our two loved ones back amongst us once again! Mrs. Ellis had to wear English clothes to keep her warm and she struggled with feeling uncomfortable in clothes she would never be seen in her homeland. Pastor Ellis had clothes that he kept for the times he would visit the UK and we all remember Pastor Ellis and his brown trousers! We recall his laugh!

The church at Wattisham made sure that in time for each furlough, Pastor and Mrs. Ellis had a car, and a place to live! As the Manse has invariably bursting with guests– there was a time when the Ellis's lived in a caravan at the back of the house of Sydney and Joan Rushbrook, senior deacon at WBC. Throughout the ministry at GH from start to finish would not have been able to continue. Sydney Rushbrook was the farmer and me

property owner of Wattisham. One third of the houses in Wattisham were owned by Sydney Rushbrook! He was a humble and godly man with a generous spirit, and he loved Gordon Hawkins. The time in a caravan in his garden was wonderful because Mr. & Mrs. Ellis became close friends with Sydney and Joan Rushbrook. Their daughter Jackie, who is a believer, recalls the time that Pastor Brian, just came out of the hospital after an appendicectomy–stayed in the home of Sydney and Joan with Tita Necy whilst he recovered. Tita Necy made everyone laugh and Pastor Brian held his side and pleaded everyone to stop laughing as it hurts when he laughs! Jackie also said that Brian and Necy were like second parents to her. She has always looked up to them and "loved them dearly", (to quote Jackie). There was a time when Brian and Necy lived next door in a house called Maybank, in the village.

My sister Lydia recalled Pastor Brian calling her Lidia, and always bringing us dried mango, and the slideshows of the work in Manila. Lydia had a great memory of Pastor Brian 'screeching' with laughter because every church he visited in the British Isles he was given quiche to eat–and he longed for ham! I remember his love of fruitcake! And then Lydia remembers the accumulation of box load of books (second-hand ones for Pastor Brian–as aid and to ship to the Philippines.

I recall more lately, feeling heartbroken that Pastor Brian came back to UK alone and he seemed frail, and a bit muddled. It made me cry. He was so dear to us as was dear Tita Necy–and very precious. We always felt desperately sad to see him go again.

> **Editor's Note:** Brian Ellis had a heart-bypass operation in 2016 and the said major operation was successful. However, by 2017 he began to have memory problems, particularly remembering recent events. His wife Necy, on the other hand, suffered from Parkinson's disease that causes unintended or uncontrollable movements, such as shaking, stiffness, and difficulty with balance and coordination. Their symptoms began gradually and worsen over time, but the love and care of the church members and friends continue, ensuring that the setting they have is quiet and without competing noise and distractions. We speak slowly and directly to each of them, giving one message at a time, and allow time for both of them to absorb the information and to form their questions. We ask prayers for these wonderful couple in their twilight years.

GEORGE CAPAQUE
Former Dean, Discipleship Training Centre in Singapore
Adjunct Faculty in Theology, Asian Theological Seminary in Manila, Philippines

By this everyone will know that you are my disciples, if you love one another" (John 13:35). More than words or teachings, *Kuya* Brian and *Ate* Necy showed me how to be a disciple of Jesus by their love for the Lord and the people of God. I was a young man then from the province coming to Manila to join the staff of Inter Varsity Christian Fellowship (IVCF). CRBC became my local church and the Ellises took me under their wings. They became like second parents to me. They offered me a comfortable bed in a room beside the EOI office during the weekend that I would stay in the church. *Ate* Necy fed me with nutritious meals which were not otherwise available to me having lived with other male staff. *Kuya* Brian taught me the ropes of ministry by letting me preach and teach during church services. When he and *Ate* Necy went for a year's furlough, he trusted me enough (and of course in the Lord's grace) to do the preaching in the young Reformed Baptist churches in Metro Manila. What I am now and have become are a confluence of God's sovereign work in my life through people He has brought to me and the experiences He has given me. *Kuya* Brian and *Ate* Necy were certainly one of those people who the Lord used to shape my Christian life and ministry.

Dean George Capaque with his wife, Dawn

Editor's Note: According to Rebecca Macapagal, Ronilo Olivares, and other founding members of CRBC, George Capaque was the first to become a co-Elder of Brian Ellis in CRBC. Earlier, George Capaque was also one of the three Deacons of CRBC, with Ronilo Olivares and Manny Gumapon.

George Capaque
July 15, 2023

DR. IAN DENSHAM
Pastor (Retired),
Droylsen Independent Church,
Greater Manchester UK
Tutor, Grace Ministerial Academy

Brian and Necy Ellis – My Dear Friends

When I was 8 and my sister was 6 years old our cousin Daphne Parker, who was 15 years older than me, went to the Philippines as a missionary with the Overseas Missionary Fellowship. My sister and I wrote to her after she had arrived in the Philippines and asked her if there was anyone we could pray for. She wrote back and suggested that we should pray for her language teacher, Necy Goco. So, for the next 20 years or so – on and off – we prayed for Necy. We never had any photos of her and had very little news (in those days there was neither internet nor mobile phones). But whenever we met anyone visiting from the Philippines we would ask if they had any news about Necy Goco.

Our family had a great interest in the missionaries who served with OMF. I cannot now remember the date when I first heard about Brian Ellis, but I did know of Pastor Don Davies. He was an evangelical Methodist Minister who came to preach at our church on one or two occasions. Later, I got to know him well after I became a pastor myself and a member of the Westminster Fellowship of ministers. Brian spent some time with Don Davies and came with Don to the Westminster Fellowship.

When Brian and Necy returned to the Philippines under the auspices of Wattisham Baptist Church I was already on his prayer letter lists. I remember well the time when he sent out the letter that announced the start of a meeting in their home in Miami Street, with a black and white photo of the event. Since then, that picture, in color, has been often shown on anniversary days at CRBC!

In 1978 I went to work for three and a half years at the Grace Baptist Mission in Abingdon. One day, Brian and Necy were in the UK and visited the mission. I knew that Brian had married a Filipina named Necy. I well remember when they walked into the office and I asked Necy whether she knew another Filipino called Necy who had been a language teacher. It was a great surprise and real joy to discover that *she* was Necy Goco whom we had been praying for over all that time! From that day on my interest and prayers for Brian received a boost of interest. I never, in my wildest dreams ever thought that I would be able to visit the Philippines.

But in the providence of God, a good friend of mine arranged for me to go and visit some work in India with which I had also supported from my childhood days. This developed into regular visits every two years or so, and Brian kept saying to me, "Why don't you come on the Philippines and visit us? It is not too far." Eventually the Lord provided the funds for me to come out to see Brian and Necy for 10 days in 1999 and to speak at the Pastors' Conference. That year was also the last year that Pastor Gordon Hawkins visited, and it was such a joy to be able to share the conference with him.

By then I was minister at Zion Church in St Ives, Cornwall. Brian and Necy had connections with Penzance Baptist Church as well, so when they were over in the UK, they were often able to visit both churches and report on the work in the Philippines. It was always a joy and privilege when they came and the church at Zion prayed for and supported the work at CRBC.

In 2004 Brian sent out a letter asking if there was anyone who would be able to come and lecture at Grace Ministerial Academy for a term on the Synoptic Gospels. I had previously completed a course on the Synoptic Gospels for my MA degree. When Brian's letter arrived, I immediately thought, "I could do that" but rejected the idea as impractical. That evening I went to take our midweek Bible Study at Zion. When we got to our prayer time, one of the members asked if I had received Brian's latest letter. She said that they were looking for a lecturer for the first term in 2005 and that she was convinced that I ought to go! I was astounded and began to raise all sorts of objections–especially saying that I did not think the church would agree anyway. But others also agreed that I should seriously consider going as "I deserved a sabbatical" they said. I thought that it was extremely unlikely as I was sure that Brian would have had lots of offers. They encouraged me to contact Brian and find out.

So, very reluctantly I emailed Brian to suggest that the church at Zion had said that they would allow me to come, but assumed he would have had far more suitable offers by now. Brian replied saying that he would be very pleased for me to come! The Lord provided the funds, and I flew out the first week of January to begin lectures. Because of the schedules I was lecturing twice a week so there was a lot of time available. This meant that with my technical and video experience I was able to film and produce a video about the work of GMA. Also, the network at the CCM office was antiquated and unreliable. So, I set about replacing the network, routers and network structure. In the three months I was there I only had one "day off" when Ismael Montejo, Gilbert McAdam and others took me to the Taal Volcano and we climbed up to the top to see the views and beauty of the Philippines. It was a great privilege to lecture, to preach in many of the churches, to take a weekend conference with Brian in Kalibo and to share in the work of God in so many places.

At the end of the visit, I was asked whether I would be willing to come again and lecture at GMA. However, the possibility of coming for three months on a regular basis was impossible, so it was suggested that perhaps I would consider coming as modular lecturer. They needed someone to lecture mainly on the Old Testament. Thus, I started to come once a year. This developed into two visits a year until 2020, when the pandemic put a stop to visits in person. I was so glad to have been able to be at the 2020 Pastors' Conference and spent much of the Conference with Brian before taking a modular on the Psalms. Since then, I have been unable to visit but have preached a few times via Zoom from the UK.

It has been a great joy and privilege to come to CRBC and GMA over the years. To come and meet with Brian and Necy over these years has been such an encouragement to me. Their work and commitment to the Philippines and the gospel here has been an inspiration to many and I am sure that the Lord has been glorified in all that they have achieved by His grace and power.

Ian M Densham

11 December 2021

Milton Keynes UK
Ingram Content Group UK Ltd.
UKHW051952131023
430521UK00006B/18

9 781312 324091